WHEN
GENEROSITY
EXCEEDS
TITHING

THE MOST GENEROUS SOULS
ARE THE MOST FLOURISHED ONES

EL AGUILA

Enrique Ruloff

Ruloff, Enrique
When Generosity Exceeds Tithing
2 Edition – March 2015

@ Copyright 2015 by Enrique Luis Ruloff
Borges 3247
1636 Olivos
Buenos Aires – Argentina
Phone: 54-11-47998533
Email: enriqueruloff@hotmail.com - fit.director@yahoo.com
Face: Enrique Ruloff – Escritor

ISBN: 978-987-33-6819-6
Deposit made according to law 11.723

Graphic Design: DaF Comunicación Gráfica dafcg@telecentro.com.ar

Edited in Argentina
March 2015 by Enrique Luis Ruloff

EL AGUILA
e d i c i o n e s

DEDICATION

*I dedicate these pages to any person,
undeniable citizen of God's Kingdom,
who with an open heart and mind,
is all set to adjust his life to our
Father's established terms.
I dedicate these pages to any person
whose heart has been transformed by God
and has become a generous giver
for the divine cause
and whose heart and mind
are open to accept the reality
of a progressive revelation
and to walk in fear to establish,
expand and make God's Kingdom
on earth grow.*

ACKNOWLEDGEMENTS

There are many people God has used in my formation, starting with my parents (I learned to pray the Lord's Prayer on my mother's lap), followed by pastors, professors, friends, brothers and sisters in faith from different places and countries, and a very important part of my life; my wife Paula, and my kids who have been my silent and active teachers all these years. I don't want to leave behind my good friend, Mauricio, with whom I've meditated on this topic about generosity many times. But, as Paul the apostle would say, written in Galatians 1:12, beyond all the people who intervened in my formation; undoubtedly the factor "revelation" is the predominant detail in my life.

By God's grace and mercy, the Holy Spirit began a work in my life many years ago. He gradually revealed aspects and details of the Gospel and the person of the triune God. As Jesus told Peter, in the face of an unmistakable answer about who Jesus was (Matthew 16), that his answer wasn't by wisdom but by divine revelation; I'm completely convinced that the same happens to all of us who today consider ourselves God's sons. We are daughters and sons by pure and absolute grace and I understand that this reality and certainty is a progressive revelation that the Holy Spirit makes, giving our spirit testimony that it is true.

Therefore, my biggest gratitude and tribute is to my Heavenly Father, for his immutable love; to his son, Jesus, who cancelled my debt with God; and to the Holy Spirit, who convinced me of my sins and now gives me his power not only to enter the Kingdom of God by grace, but to be able to stay in that same grace, and that way gradually grow in the knowledge of who He is and of what he has revealed for His sons. To talk about kingdom and be able to understand a little about it, means that an important torrent of God's grace has been poured in us. I feel privileged by that. Thank you (Abba) Daddy.

I can't forget to mention, and I do it with gratitude, the unconditional support from Pilgrim Church in New Jersey. Thanks to their main pastor and their pastor in the missions area. They have trusted in my work for many years, and they have done it again this time. Thank you, may the Lord reward the effort you make for His church in Latin America.

PROLOGUE

This book, which content surprised me, since I had never thought about tithe in these terms, isn't written by a materialistic and voracious pastor, who wanders through life lightly preaching the theology of prosperity. Conversely, it's the revelation that, coming from the Holy Spirit, a man, known by his Christian testimony and above all for the consistency of his theological knowledge, received.

Enrique Ruloff is a pastor who's sensitive to the guidance of the Holy Spirit and absolutely respectful of the Bible. These virtues position him in a serious and reliable seat of honor. Hence to this, the reading of this book must be taken as a divine guidance that will make us reach new levels in our spiritual walk, and as a challenge to believe in the Lord's multiple promises related to generosity.

Have you ever thought that, as a result of your growth and

maturity in faith, the law of tithe could become a limit for your increasing generosity?

When you walk through the pages of this literary work, all those Christians who have reached maturity will feel the blessed impulse to rethink the way in which they pay God for so many received benefits. And that will open new doors of revelation and blessings for you.

Marcelo Laffitte
Writer and Journalist

TESTIMONY

My story with the tithe issue is fascinating. When I was new in faith, I read William Colgate's testimony, maker of the well-known toothpastes and toiletries, and also owner of the American company "Caterpillar", which manufactures machinery and motors. These men appeared to be increasing their donations for the Lord from tithing, in the beginning, then 20%, later 50% of their earnings, to finally keeping only the 10% for living.

When I heard of these stories I couldn't help thinking: "These people lie and exaggerate or they really do have a lot of faith". Turned out it was the second option and that challenged me. I decided not only to grow spiritually but also make my generosity grow for the Lord. He said to me: "Test me... Test me". And little by little I tested him. It took me thirty years, and since 2007, I give God 90% of my earnings and live with the remaining 10%... and I've never lived so well! I have some companies in Venezuela and Argentina that today allow me to achieve, in six months, CCN projects that would have taken six years or more. And they are companies God prospers.

I wish many could experience that giving the Lord is the best way of receiving, because there's no doubt that "the generous soul will be prospered" (Proverbs 11:25).

Rev. Raul Avila
Christian Center for the Nations President (CCN)
Caracas, Venezuela.

CONTENT

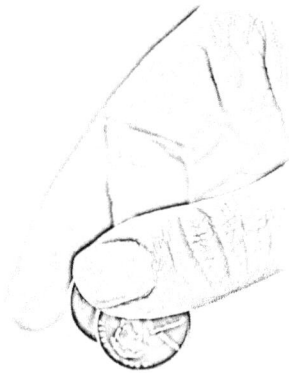

INTRODUCTION

When we look at Christ's church, we can identify a progressive revelation in many aspects. Many years ago, not many people had access to theological education, but today, through different seminaries and biblical institutes, training is available to more people, either in person, semi-distance, Internet, distance learning, etc.

If we look at the strategies used for the church's growth, until a few years ago, sermons were reduced to the pulpit, which was within four walls. Today, not only we can continue that strategy, but we can also add it to the media, such as: radio, TV, Internet, Facebook, Twitter, etc.

When I was a child (not many years ago) the liturgy of many congregations was reduced to some hymns, a sermon, tithes and then back home. However, these past few years we have experienced a renovation in this aspect and in many cases we have incorporated technology as an important part of our services.

From mobilizing as leaders in horses, carriages and trains to take the gospel to other latitudes; for the last few decades, many of us have been mobilizing in fast cars, buses with excellent on-board services and aircrafts in case of longer distances or cross borders of our country.

The ecclesiology has changed throughout our continents. From having churches where the ministry was better known than the pastor, to having other gifts which are being developed and taking important interferences in the church's government. Since a very few years, more space and support has been given to the prophetic and apostolic ministries, not only through words, but also with financial support.

The missions have undergone profound changes. For many decades, local churches, through their mission agencies, have sent missionaries to different parts of the world to carry the good news of Jesus. But recently and nowadays, the idea or vision of raising autochthonous leaders has been on the works, not only to reduce costs, but also to potentiate local leadership.

We have undergone many good changes, but facing each new proposal, the church has demonized the idea, to later accept it and use it. It should be noted that some leaders, who still live, when TV emerged, treated the receiver as a "devil's box", to later no only use that mean, but to also take possession of the imaging stations to communicate the message of the good news.

Above all the positive and necessary changes, there are a few i-ssues left to solve. As a church, we are still in debt. We haven't come to an agreement, neither internationally nor locally, about the role of women in the church. There hasn't been an establish-ment or unified posture about ethic issues, as euthanasia, abortion, civil and religious union of same sex couples, cloning, in vitro fertility, etc.

One of the subjects I want to address in this book, which the church hasn't dealt with nor is updated, is the economic or financial issues for the support of the mission. In the official religion, alms are the every-day bread, since there isn't a big necessity of the believers' contribution because the government, through the people's taxes, assigns a percentage for the maintenance of the official religion. Churches with more traditional aspects, as in neighborhood clubs, for many years have sustained a social quote or membership to obtain the services of baptism, wedding and burial. In more charismatic and evangelical churches, tithing, as an obligation, has been the Trojan horse to sustain and expand the Kingdom and in many cases to enlarge the arks of the same leaders.

Beginning this new millennium, it is essential that as a church we look over this subject in the light of the Scriptures, especially from the New Testament. We can't pretend to establish changes in the leadership and in the ecclesiastic model taking the New Testament as a source of principal inspiration, but when it comes to talk and teach about stewardship principles we just stay with the Old Testament without observing what Jesus, the disciples and the first Christians learnt and taught about it.

This book, "When generosity exceeds tithing" is an approach to the issue of gifts. But before you think that as an author I don't believe in the principle of tithing. Let me tell you that I simply believe that after some time of getting to know God, we should be contributing more than that. But for that to happen, we need to get rid of certain ties and traditions and open the gate, or remove the ceiling's limits, so that the Kingdom's citizens can enjoy and benefit from the acts of generosity that transcend those imposed and sustained limits through decades.

Genesis 41 to 47 tells us about the story of the Pharaoh's dream about the seven fat cows and the seven lean cows, as well as the seven stuffed spikes and the seven spikes with no grains. In the dream, the lean cows eat the fat cows and the empty spikes eat the stuffed ones. Joseph, receiving God's revelation, interprets this dreams telling the Pharaoh that both dreams were only one thing and that the fact that they were two meant that it was decreed by God for it to happen, and soon.

After interpreting that seven good years of abundance would come; followed by seven bad years of much shortage, Joseph gave the Pharaoh a strategy telling him to harvest as much as he could during the seven years of abundance. By the second year of drought, Joseph bought all the Egyptian's lands in exchange for seeds to plant and then established that a fifth of the harvest, that is to say a 20% of it, would be taken by the Pharaoh. (Gn. 47:24). After the abundance and drought years were over, the contribution of the 20% for the government was established (Gn. 47:26). Jesus talks about giving as gathering treasures in heaven, as saving seeds in God's barn. As Christians we never think about the possibility that in times of abundance we could give more than the 10% so that in times of shortage we could give less. It was always posed as a fixed percentage, not negotiable and even damned if we didn't comply with that ten percent.

The proposal of this book is not only to share other parameters in regards to our economic investment in the Kingdom, but also to make a contribution for a wider administration of the resources God gives us, not only personally but also as a church. The reader will be challenged to be able to grow in his giving without putting a limit. Welcome to this adventure, and let yourself be surprised by God.

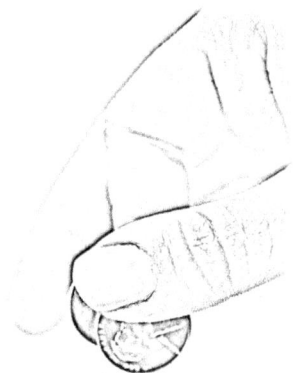

1 - THE CHURCH
OF THE FUTURE

The Church of the future is a church with no denominational limits. It's a church centered in the person of Jesus, with extended arms towards a needed and hopeless society. When we read the Scriptures, we learn that Jesus' vision about church is bigger than buildings, structures, committees or denominations. We see that he dreamt about a Kingdom composed by men and women, regardless races, cultures or ages, co-governing on earth under the Holy Spirit's leadership.

John the apostle, while he was exiled in the Patmos Island, had a vision of the church of the end of times. The veil of eternity was briefly moved and he could spiritually see what we will soon physically see. In Revelations 7:9-12 God records it like this:

> "After this I looked, and there before me was a great multitude that no one could count, from every nation, tribe, people and language, standing before

the throne and before the Lamb. They were wearing
white robes and were holding palm branches in their
hands. And they cried out in a loud voice: «Salva-
tion belongs to our God, who sits on the throne, and
to the Lamb» All the angels were standing around
the throne and around the elders and the four living
creatures. They fell down on their faces before the
throne and worshiped God, saying: «Amen! Praise
and glory and wisdom and thanks and honor and
power and strength be to our God for ever and ever.
Amen!»"

Pitifully as a church we have remained stagnant. The e-nemy has distracted us with personal projects, big buildings and for many years he has silenced our voice. We have played more of a defensive role in society and not offensive. When we read the gospel in Matthew, in chapter 16, Jesus declares: *"And I tell you that you are Peter, and on this rock I will build my church, and the gates of Hades will not overcome it."*

We all have a door in our house that is basically used to defend ourselves from the enemies. Jesus says that it's the same door of hell that will not be able to stand because His church will break in and plunder those who are captive.

But for many centuries the church has hidden behind the door, has been enclosed within the four walls, has developed nice programs and has sung beautiful choirs, while the enemy has been at ease outside.

The church of the future is a brave church; it's a church full of God's spirit, and it will overflow in His love and power and will break in the enemy's camp to rescue those who are prisoners, captives, blind, sick and hopeless. Jesus started his ministry in Nazareth, saying in Luke 4:18-19:

> *"The Spirit of the Lord is on me, because he has anointed me to proclaim good news to the poor. He has sent me to proclaim freedom for the prisoners and recovery of sight for the blind, to set the oppressed free, to proclaim the year of the Lord's favor."*

To become who we should be, we need to change. It is said that a definition of insanity is to expect different results by doing the same over and over again. We can't be the church of the future that God dreamt about unless we are prepared to change.

Worldwide culture has changed

On Vineyard Church's website, Pastor Ken Wilson wrote the following:

"The church exists for the sake of those who are far from God. We are called to take the kingdom's gospel to every corner of the world and to all creation, faithfully translating Jesus' message in languages and ways that are relevant to the diverse cultures and people. As a movement we aim to plant churches that are culturally, locally and internationally relevant. Every congregation is encouraged to reach people from their community who haven't been reached by the gospel. Therefore, we promote a creative, entrepreneurial and innovative approach to the ministry that is faithful to Jesus and wishes to reach those who are far from God."

We need to change our monastery mentality for a missionary mentality. Culture is a combination of lifestyles and manners, knowledge in a time or a social group.

In 1 Corinthians 9:19-23, Apostle Paul writes:

> *"Though I am free and belong to no one, I have made myself a slave to everyone, to win as many as possible. To the Jews I became like a Jew, to win the Jews. To those under the law I became like one under the law (though I myself am not under the law), so as to win those under the law. To those not having the law I became like one not having the law (though I am not free from God's law but am under Christ's law), so as to win those not having the law. To the weak I became weak, to win the weak. I have become all things to all people so that by all possible means I might save some. I do all this for the sake of the gospel that I may share in its blessings."*

At first sight we could think Paul was a hypocrite who wore different masks, but in reality he was passionate for the things God is passionate about, that are people. Paul wanted, by any mean, to try to reach the biggest quantity of people possible. In another moment, he would write to the church in Rome, in Romans 12:2 saying: *"Do not conform to the pattern of this world, but be transformed by the renewing of your mind. Then you will be able to test and approve what God's will is—his good, pleasing and perfect will."*

We need to understand the cultural changes we have suffered in the last decades:

- Pre-Modern Era: In those times, the priest was the judge, father and referent in the community. What the priest said was holy word.
- Modern Era: After the industrial revolution, the scientist o-

ccupied the priest's role. If a scientist said it, then humanity believed it. Thus faith was replaced for what was seen.

- Post-Modern Era: In our times the rock star is who determines values, culture and the principles of life in a society. It doesn't matter whether it's true or not, if something works and is practical, we use it. The "I feel" has taken the place of the "I believe".

Statistics predict that by the year 2050, 1 out of 4 people in the United States will be Hispanic. This means that around 100.000.000 people will be from Hispanic origins and will speak Spanish. Probably by that time there will be more Hispanic people in the United States than in the rest of Latin America. It will be a new field for evangelism. It is believed that by the same year the 80% of the worldwide population will live in big urbanizations. Nowadays, that's the percentage of Argentineans living in cities. Some scholars believe that in the next few years, Argentina will have an immigration of thousands of people and many of them will be Chinese, European and North Americans who will escape xenophobia.

Globalization has gotten us in communication circuits that were unthinkable in years past. Today a citizen from Buenos Aires is more communicated with another citizen in China, Japan, United States or Mexico than with his own countrymen.

As a church we can't be left out and lock ourselves in our little parishes and gather firewood for our own barbecue. As the evangelist John Wesley would say, the world is our chapel and we need to develop our ministries with the Kingdom's vision. We can no longer think locally, it's essential to think globally.

Perception about Christians has changed

Trademarks characterize the marketing world. Just by seeing the symbols we are able to know which product it is. Children see a big, yellow M, and they automatically relate it to hamburgers and fries.

What is our brand as Christians? Love should be the trademark for Jesus' church. At least that's how Jesus saw and sees His church.

The Barna investigation group surveyed a group of young non-Christians aged from 16 to 29 years old, to know how they see Christians. This is how they see us:

- Anti-homosexuals – 91%
- Judge others – 87%
- Hypocrites – 85%
- Outdated – 78%
- Very involved in politics – 75%
- Doesn't understand reality – 72%
- Insensitive to others – 70%
- Boring – 68%
- Don't accept people of other faiths – 64%
- Confusing – 61%

Summarized, the world sees the church as an irrelevant organization for these times. However, God has seen and gestated it like something transcendent. Jesus declared that as a church we are the salt of the earth and the light of this world.

As salt we are agents of corruption prevention and we also spice up life. Christians should be the most attractive, humorous, helpful and hopeful people. The Bible tells us about new heavens and new earth. We will discuss this further in the next chapter.

As light we are called to illuminate a world that is in darkness and that walk towards a cliff. As a politician would say: *"When we took the country, it was on the edge of a cliff. Today we can certainly say that we have taken a step forward."* If salt loses its ability to salt and light loses its ability to illuminate, then there's no sense in their existence. Salt in a saltshaker is useless. No matter the amount of energy accumulated inside giant transformers, if they can't illuminate and make that energy useful for the community where we live, then it stops being something useful.

We are not called to illuminate where there's light, we need to get out of the four walls and get involved in politics, education, laws, etc., because while we are playing church and disputing internal charges that do not make a change in our society, the enemy is outside occupying all the relevant charges.

It's true that we have to pray, but it's also true that we need to act. "Pray to God and keep your powder dry", says the saying. We need to encourage our youth to study, to take several university courses, so that through education they can occupy relevant positions and affect, from short to medium term, the culture, education, laws and politics of a nation.

For many years we have been satisfied with the unction, we have demanded the fire; but we have forgotten that the fire without firewood is just an artificial fire that today burns and tomorrow extinguishes. Calvino and the other reformers set up their reform project about education and projected it on a long term. Let us not forget that Jesus was firstly and foremost a teacher, then a preacher and then a healer.

Essential changes so that Christians can make an impact the worldwide culture

Writer Andy crouch on one of his books wrote: *"It's not enough to criticize culture, consume culture, and trust culture. We were created to create culture. What are you creating?"* We all create something, because it's in our DNA. The question for us today is: What are we creating as people, as a family and specially, as a church? God has called us to get involved in one of the biggest businesses in the universe, which is to establish God's Kingdom on earth.

Actually, we all know the Lord's Prayer and one of the first petitions Jesus taught us to pray in Matthew 6:10 is: "your kingdom come, your will be done, on earth as it is in heaven". We are called as a church to recreate heaven on Earth and make this world more habitable, where justice, equity and peace reign. God hasn't aborted his Eden project. Although we're living in an interval, truth is that His project is still prevailing.

Some handy steps we can take into account:

- **Connect with the neighborhood**. Connect with people who don't know Jesus. It's good to spend some time with brothers and sisters in faith, but it's necessary to develop bonds with those who don't know Jesus so we can own the right to be heard by them.
- **Serve with compassion.** What necessities do people have? The word 'mercy' is the combination of two Greek words that mean 'misery' and 'heart'. We are called to put our hearts in others' misery. A distinctive feature in Jesus' ministry was his compassion, since he saw people as sheeps with no shepherd. And that compassion was the motor of all the miracles He performed.

- **Generate a community of love**. Jesus said the world would believe in Him when we loved one another. The German preacher, Dietrich Bonhoeffer said: "A church is a church when it exists for those who don't belong to it". I usually say that the church is the only organization that exists for the benefit of those who aren't members.
- **Ask the Holy Spirit to Light us with passion for God and compassion for others.** The reformer John Knox told God: *"Give me Scotland or I die"*. May our prayer be *"Lord, give us our city or country, or we die"*.

We notice the word 'culture' has the same roots the word 'cultivate' has. And the word 'relevant' is similar to the word 'e-levate'. In other words, God is calling us as church to stand up and cultivate, to stand up to cultivate connection, compassion and community. It doesn't matter how many habitant our city has, truth is that there are millions of lonely lives that need to find a community environment.

God gives us the grace to embrace the church of the future, which gives us the courage to take the correct decisions to go from being obsolete institution to being vital organisms and agents of change.

God gives us the grace to create a nation with the Kingdom's mentality, with its hearts burning for a world that's lost and committed to transform men and women from every ethnicity, nation and culture, so that one day they'll be in the presence of the Lamb who has been sacrificed for us, giving Him all the love, gratitude and worship He deserves. I want to be one of those John saw in Revelations 7, what about you? If we had within reach the Google Heart of eternity we would see ourselves where John saw us.

"After this I looked, and there before me was a great multitude that no one could count, from every nation, tribe, people and language, standing before the throne and before the Lamb. They were wearing white robes and were holding palm branches in their hands."

Pray: *"God, let your Holy Spirit make use of your Word in our lives and make us able to accept the challenge of getting involved in the expansion of Your Kingdom, with a heart, soul, spirit and mind like yours. In Jesus' name, amen."*

2 - TOWARDS A CHURCH WITH AN APOSTOLIC MENTAL

When we look at the birth, growth and extension of the church, we discover that it has to do with:

A DIVINE PURPOSE: Ephesians 5:24-26 *"Now as the church submits to Christ, so also wives should submit to their husbands in everything. Husbands, love your wives, just as Christ loved the church and gave himself up for her to make her holy, cleansing her by the washing with water through the word"*.

A DIVINE DESIGN: Ephesians 3:10-11 *"His intent was that now, through the church, the manifold wisdom of God should be made known to the rulers and authorities in the heavenly realms, according to his eternal purpose that he accomplished in Christ Jesus our Lord"*.

A DIVINE TASK: Matthew 16:18 *"And I tell you that you are Peter, and on this rock I will build my church, and the gates of Hades will not overcome it"*.

A psalmist declared saying, *"Unless the LORD builds the house, the builders' labor in vain"* (Psalms 127:1). It's been many years since God created it, and not only created, but also supporting it during all these centuries. This leads me to agree with the fact that the church is the only instrument God has to EXPRESS, ESTABLISH and EXTEND His Kingdom on earth.

Some time ago I met with a good friend, Pastor Basilio Patiño, who has shared with me most of the content in this chapter. We use to preach in the same church in New Jersey, United States; and in one of my visits there, we met up and talked about the changes we were going through and will go through during the next few years. It's a great blessing in my life knowing him.

We are seeing one of the most dramatic changes in the church's history after the Protestant Reform. The change is radical, sudden, reformist, fast and renewing. There are times ahead when God will carry out what Jeremiah 1:12 says, that He hurries to see his word fulfilled. Probably, what took others ten years to accomplish, will take us three years.

Time ago I accidentally met a man with whom I shared a three hour flight. I had the opportunity to talk to him about the gospel, he accepted Jesus and God surprised me when in a very short time this man Ariel, could understand the aspects of generous tithing, the sowing and reaping principles, as well as other aspects of the spiritual battle that's released within us once we know Jesus and need to give up old idols. These basic issues have taken many years for Christians to understand.

Experts tell us that our society is rediscovering itself every three or five years. Two or three new models of thought and behavior are produced every decade, which bring different variants in the collective behavior. That is to say that tomorrow came yesterday. Basically there are six areas where the Church should review and redefine its BEING, KNOWING and OBEYING God's call, to be relevant to an indifferent society that qualifies it as obsolete and irrelevant.

Proper Structure

By this I mean the kind of government and administration that's covered to protect and promote the ministries and that's not a lid to hide them, suffocate them and put them out. There are many churches whose commissions exist to abort projects more than to support them to be executed.

The church has to be a space where Relationships are more important than Rules, where Personal Confidence is more valuable than Organizational Control. The structure of an Apostolic Church's government encourages RELATIONSHIPS OF PACTS, RELATIONSHIPS Of POWER, RELATIONSHIPS OF PURPOSE and RELATIONSHIPS OF PRINCIPLES.

The structure of the church's government can't continue being handled by a pastoral and business perspective where the figure of a hierarchical boss is seen more than that of a Kingdom's prophet. It's essential that human government, whatever it's form, is replaced by divine government. The old pastoral model of a rural church has to be changed to an apostolic and directional model. We need to train men and women with urban mentalities, with a deep love for the people who lives in cities.

Effective Strategy

We need to activate the unction of Issachar's sons, who

understood the times and knew what they had to do for the battle, whose brothers followed their advice and direction (1 Chronicles 12:32). As pastors and leaders we need that; we need God to give us the spirit of revelation, to understand times, so that we can interpret the Kairos of God.

The church must be liturgically innovative, that is that the form and content of worship is not machined; but **reverently** exalts God, **influentially** edifies the believer and **appealingly** reaches the unbeliever.

The church must be spiritually renewing, that is to stay on the crest of the wave of God's moving, or otherwise it atrophies and fossilizes. This doesn't mean we have to run after every a-ppearing fashion, but it does mean we have to discern whether the wave's from God for the whole church or something particular for a certain congregation or region. It's necessary to change the pachyderm mentality, that is, layers that cover our spiritual skin and blocks the Spirit's fresh operation, otherwise we will be perpetuating a rigid organization and not strengthening a living organism. Knowing the gospel for many years does not necessarily mean we are mature Christians, it does sometimes mean that we are stubborn Christians.

The church must be socially transforming, so its influence through its prophetic actions should break the prevailing systems of inequity and injustice. We can't go out to the streets with similar protests to the political parties or non-governmental organizations. Our tools and strategies must be different.

We have to be wise to change the container without altering the content. Neither idolizing the methods nor living from past glories. It's necessary to break obsolete systems and check the projects to change the unproductive ones and not keep them because of tradition.

Our responsibility is to train with a purpose and not entertain with programs. "If you want to see what have never seen, start doing what you have never done".

Conquering Spirit

We must return to yesterday's fire, not to the ashes! The revival of the present is not lighted with yesterday's ashes, but with today's fire, blowing with the faith of tomorrow. We must only go back to the past to learn from our mistakes and not to wallow in them since God has forgiven us. We can't allow the past to mortgage our present and future.

It's vital to keep the right attitude, not a nostalgic spirit focused on what we did in the past, but a militant and combative action, which leads to take possession of the legacy that has been given to us.

We need to leave a prepared platform so that the next generation of leaders can be able to go further than where we went, do more than what we did and have more than what we achieved. As David did, we must serve our generation according to God's purposes. We must rethink what kind of church we want our children to inherit.

We can't repeat the bad habits and mistakes our predecessors had (intrigue, envy, jealousy, politicking and ministerial rivalry). It would be foolish to fall into the same trap as those we have criticized many times because of their mistakes, but we have not imitated their successes. We can't be so naïve to believe that

older people did everything wrong and that we are doing everything correctly. Not everything that's old is bad and not everything that's new is good. We must be wise to discern what can be
retained and discard what does not contribute.

It's our responsibility to cultivate an attitude of progress
and significance, that can define higher goals, as well as to keep
steadier principles that can forge clearer models. We need God
to give us his spirit of discernment so that we can elaborate new
strategies without negotiating our principles.

Contextualized Style

We need to apply the ETERNAL PRINCIPLES in Modern
Methods, operating according to the time, place and culture. We
shouldn't be afraid of the diverse manifestations of God's multiform grace, and we should accept that even in the contemporary
forms that are not of our liking, God works and blesses. Today we
can't pretend to have our central meetings on Sunday mornings,
because the reality is that many people, because of work or study,
need to find other days and times to grow in faith. In recent times,
the emerging church has appeared, which is slowly gaining space
and presenting new alternatives of worshiping and serving God.

We can't keep talking with smoke signals to a generation
that navigates the internet, it's necessary to know and learn the
languages and codes our society uses to communicate with each
other, so that we can share with them the message of the Gospel in
an understandable and adequate way.

The Word declares that these are times of restoration and
refreshment, Luke says on Acts 3:19-21 *"Repent, then, and turn
to God, so that your sins may be wiped out, that times of refreshing*

may come from the Lord, and that he may send the Messiah, who has been appointed for you—even Jesus. Heaven must receive him until the time comes for God to restore everything, as he promised long ago through his holy prophets".

But it's also a time of removal, where mobile things will be removed so that the unshaken can be stablished as said by the author on Hebrews 12:27-28 *"The words 'once more' indicate the removing of what can be shaken—that is, created things—so that what cannot be shaken may remain. Therefore, since we are receiving a kingdom that cannot be shaken, let us be thankful, and so worship God acceptably with reverence and awe".*

This is why we shouldn't see the Apostolic Dimension as a temporary movement or a new evangelical wave; we should see it as the possible establishment of Christ's government for his church; which was directly constituted by the risen and ascended Christ, who distributed his anointing in five ministries for His church; as Paul declares in Ephesians 4:11-12 *"So Christ himself gave the apostles, the prophets, the evangelists, the pastors and teachers, to equip his people for works of service, so that the body of Christ may be built up".*

Kingdom Economy

For many centuries the church has stayed with a model of the Old Testament in the area of economics. We have fluctuated monthly fees models, special offerings, preparation of food for its later sale, raffles, tithes, mega-tithes, covenants and hyper covenants. The truth is that it's necessary and urgent to re-read the New Testament and be able to discover that both, Jesus and the apostle Paul, suggested other alternative.

In the next chapters I will expand on an integrative proposal on this issue, but as a preview I'll tell you that in the Old Testament, the 10% belonged to God and the 90% to the Israelite. But in the New Testament the 100% belongs to God and he gives us the responsibility and privilege of generously tithing according to how He has prospered us weekly. It should also be recalled, and we will deepen more in the next chapter, God is the one who gives us the seed to sow.

Visionary Approach

By this we mean the perspective the church has to keep based on four pillars:

Formative Theology

We must change the spirit and content of our message; activating the Word of Revelation. Traditionally it's been said that the 'rock' that Jesus refers to in Mathew 16 is Peter the apostle, therefore, the apostolic succession or the popes. For centuries, the evangelical church held that the 'rock' refers to Jesus. But if we read the whole context we will see that in the previous chapter, Jesus answers Peter that his correct answer wasn't because of his intelligence, but because the Father had revealed it. Now I ask, could it be that the "revelation" is the rock upon which Jesus' church is built on? Paul, writing to the Galatians, tells them that he didn't receive the gospel he preaches because of men's wisdom, but because Jesus revealed it to him. Having this in mind, we can say we need to activate the Word of Revelation, or the Rhema to go from:

- Jesus the Suffering Lamb to Christ the Triumphant Lion;
- The cross to the crown;
- The baptism in water as the goal of evangelism to baptism in

the Spirit as a mean of preaching the Gospel;
- Fear of evil to assuming the power we have over the devil;
- A rigid tradition to a renewed anointing;
- The frivolous liturgy to spontaneous worship;
- Condemnation of sin to victory over sin;
- Legalism and debauchery to liberating grace.

We must be open to examine everything, retain the good and discard the bad. Because we lack a positive attitude and a spirit of diligent research, like the believers in Berea; we have rejected theological riches and valuable contributions from different movements in the history of church. We have to bathe the baby, but not throw it away with the dirty water.

Dynamic Ecclesiology

We must have the training and projection of a church that comes out from the desert to possess the land. Unfortunately we have acted like the Israel from the desert, who had achieved liberation from Egypt by the hands of Moses, but in their minds they could never experience freedom, and therefore they died free but with a slave mentality. Many times the same happens with the church, we've been freed from our sins and debts, but we act as if we were still salves. We must be a church that operates beyond the four walls and can be influential in the world, without the world influencing in it; since it knows how to discover its Purpose, Develop its Potential, Define its Participation and Broadcast its Preaching.

Positive Eschatology

Christ's true church in not a church that keeps a fatalist mentality, since it knows Christ reigns, not the devil. It's a church that looks like the Perfect Man, fully mature and capable of possessing what Christ already won. It's a church that knows that it's the Lamb's Wife who enters victoriously through the main entrance and not the world's servile Cinderella who runs out history's back door. We are called to knock down the gates of hell and not to hide behind it in fear of the enemy.

It's good to remember that the last chapter of the story is not death, violence or the planet's final hecatomb; the last chapter has new heavens, new lands where there won't be any crying, nor pain, nor death. God never aborted the project of Eden. It remains in force. We're living in an interval, but there will come a day where God will physically and visibly resume that project. Meanwhile we are transiting the story of salvation.

Multiform Ministry

Today more than ever, people are hopeless. During the last few years the world has been shaken by earthquakes, tsunamis, deaths, volcanoes, floods, economic crisis, etc., and together with that, the faith of many has been tested. The foundations of the earth were shaken and the values of many were tested.

As a relevant church we need to stand in the gap and intercede for those who are going through some kind of necessity, because it's by these details that we prove God is real, that He exists, that He loves us and that He has a plan for our lives.

When the church prays, God works. When we invite the Holy Spirit to glorify Christ in our lives, miracles happen, lives are changed, the oppressed are freed, and the hopeless begin to see the world with different eyes.

God calls us to raise our hands and cry out for His presence to transform us. The preacher Charles Spurgeon once said, *"If the spirit of prayer is not in the people, the minister can preach like an angel, but he can't expect success. If the spirit of prayer is not in a church there can be wealth, there can be talent, there can be a certain grade of effort, there can be a big infrastructure, but the Lord is not there. That men pray is as sure proof of the presence of God, as the rise of the thermometer is evidence of increased temperature. By measuring the Nilometer the rising water in the Nile, also predicts the amount of the harvest in Egypt. Thus, the prayer meeting is a 'grace-mometer', and from it we can judge the size of God's work in a place. If God is near a church, this must pray, and if He's not here, one of the first signs of His absence will be the laziness in prayer".*

Pray: *"Father, give us the grace and perseverance to seek you and be agents of change in such way that your church can adjust to the necessary changes and be a church with an apostolic mentality. In Jesus's name. Amen".*

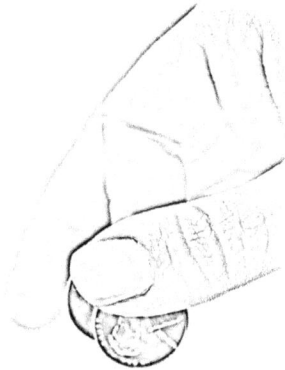

3 - CITIZENS WITH KINGDOM'S ECONOMY

When we read the biblical text we find anonymous stories. Some of these unknown stories that appear in the gospels are unknown friends of Jesus; like the one who borrowed him the garden at the mount of the olives, or the one who lent him the upper chambers to celebrate the last supper with his disciples or the one who borrowed the donkey for his triumphal entry into Jerusalem.

As to this last story, the biblical text tells us that the disciples went to untie the donkey and while they did so, the owner asked them: "What are you doing?" to what they simply answered: "The master needs it". Facing this answer he didn't anything else and the disciples took the donkey. It would be a very laudable of us if we had the same feeling towards everything he has given us; which by the way, and not less importantly, is a butler's right attitude.

In this section of the book I would like to emphasize some principles of stewardship in general, so that we can understand that everything we have comes from God and one day we will have to be held accountable for this. I will refer to two passages, one from the Old Testament and other from the New Testament.

Psalms 24:1-2
> *"The earth is the LORD's, and everything in it, the world, and all who live in it; for he founded it on the seas and established it on the waters".*

Matthew 25:14-30
> *"Again, it will be like a man going on a journey, who called his servants and entrusted his wealth to them. To one he gave five bags of gold, to another two bags, and to another one bag, each according to his ability. Then he went on his journey. The man who had received five bags of gold went at once and put his money to work and gained five bags more. So also, the one with two bags of gold gained two more. But the man who had received one bag went off, dug a hole in the ground and hid his master's money. After a long time the master of those servants returned and settled accounts with them. The man who had received five bags of gold brought the other five. 'Master,' he said, 'you entrusted me with five bags of gold. See, I have gained five more.' His master replied, 'Well done, good and faithful servant! You have been faithful with a few things; I will put you in charge of many things. Come and share your master's happiness!' The man with two bags of gold also came. 'Master,' he said, 'you entrusted me with two bags of gold; see, I have gained two more.' His master replied, 'Well done, good and faithful servant! You have been faithful with a few things;*

I will put you in charge of many things. Come and share your master's happiness!' Then the man who had received one bag of gold came. 'Master,' he said, 'I knew that you are a hard man, harvesting where you have not sown and gathering where you have not scattered seed. So I was afraid and went out and hid your gold in the ground. See, here is what belongs to you.' His master replied, 'You wicked, lazy servant! So you knew that I harvest where I have not sown and gather where I have not scattered seed? Well then, you should have put my money on deposit with the bankers, so that when I returned I would have received it back with interest. "So take the bag of gold from him and give it to the one who has ten bags. For whoever has, will be given more, and they will have in abundance. Whoever does not have, even what they have will be taken from them. And throw that worthless servant outside, into the darkness, where there will be weeping and gnashing of teeth".

I will try to focus the subject of stewardship or administration in main items; but before I would like to define what a steward is. A steward is someone who takes care or manages others' goods, that is their owner's goods.

God owns everything

According to the parable of the talents told by Jesus in Matthew 25, God is the owner of everything; of the goods and even of men and we are simply temporary users who one day will have to be held accountable before God about how we did the job. That day, believers will be rewarded while the negligent will receive a punishment. God is the owner of everything for three main reasons:

Rights of creation

The Genesis tells us that in the beginning God created heaven and earth and that being empty and untidy, God filled it and arranged it. At the end He created a man to govern and multiply on earth, but He never gave him the right of possession, but of usufruct. Some time ago, my parents decided to arrange the papers for their goods, they went before a notary and made a testament putting each of their children on it as heirs of their goods, but under a law of usufruct; which means that while they are alive their children can't decide upon those goods. Although those goods will be ours, my parents are still legal owners and can do whatever they want with them. The same happens with God, we can manage, multiply, etc., but it's good to remind ourselves that he is the owner and not us.

Rights of preservation

When God finished creating the earth he didn't abandon it. Psalm 104 is a hymn where the psalmist highlights the preoccupation and preservation of nature by God, who takes care of everything through His creative Word. Paul describes this reality, writing to the church in Colossae, where he declares: *"The Son is the image of the invisible God, the firstborn over all creation. For in him all things were created: things in heaven and on earth, visible and invisible, whether thrones or powers or rulers or authorities; all things have been created through him and for him. He is before all things, and in him all things hold together."* (Colossians 1:15-17)

Why is there violence, confusion, environmental contamination, disease, disasters, etc.? Not because God has abandoned the world, but because we have abandoned God. Men decided to be free, and perverted himself and became a slave of sin and Satan.

Rights of redemption

Men's sin brought death, slavery, evil; but God decided to buy us and paid for us the price of His Son and reconciled us to him. Therefore, everything belongs to God, even ourselves. In 1 Chronicles 29:13-16 God declares: *"Now, our God, we give you thanks, and praise your glorious name. But who am I, and who are my people, that we should be able to give as generously as this? Everything comes from you, and we have given you only what comes from your hand. We are foreigners and strangers in your sight, as were all of our ancestors. Our days on earth are like a shadow, without hope. LORD our God, all this abundance that we have provided for building you a temple for your Holy Name comes from your hand, and all of it belongs to you"*.

This passage amazes me every time. It's a text that puts us well within the Kingdom's economy. There's no doubt God is the owner of everything and we are mere administrators.

We are temporary users

Job, in the midst of his crisis, expressed himself in the following way: *"Naked I came from my mother's womb, and naked I will depart. The LORD gave and the LORD has taken away; may the name of the LORD be praised"* (Job 1:21). If we analyze our lives and be honest with ourselves a little bit, we will realize we have received many things from God, such as:

Life

We have received the life we have from God as a loan; it's not ours, and therefore we have to take care of it. This life is somehow a rehearsal for eternity. Genesis 2:7 declares: *"Then the LORD God formed a man from the dust of the ground and breathed into his nostrils the breath of life, and the man became a living being"*.

Abilities

Every ability we receive, either by inheritance, intellectual, artistic or manual, comes from God and therefore we have to manage them properly.

Opportunities

God gives us opportunities to advance in life, to study, to make money or form a family, and we have to take careful and faithful advantage of them. In a sense, we are all privileged beings.

Health

Health is a gift that many times we don't value and somehow believe we deserve. Generally when we lose our health or it begins to deteriorate, we realize its value. Sometime diseases help us grow, as in Hellen Keller's case, who, even blind, wrote amazing hymns, or the biblical presenter, William Barclay, who even though he was blind, wrote many books.

Family

Family is a gift from God, whether it's beautiful or conflictive. Therefore we have to find the key to fulfill ourselves and, as a family, try to coexist in peace and harmony.

Influences

We all influence for good or for bad. If we understand that God want to use our influences for the good of others or for the extension of his Kingdom and we do so, we will find a source of happiness. The influences we have shouldn't be a reason for personal pride, but a reason to thank God and use them faithfully.

Material goods

The author of 1 Chronicles 29:14 states: *"But who am I, and who are my people, that we should be able to give as generously as this? Everything comes from you, and we have given you only what comes from your hand"*. Everything's from God: our house, money, car, family, career, abilities, etc. Therefore, there's no place for pride and vainglory.

Time

Each of us has 24 hours or 1440 minutes per day and as good stewards we should use them properly and productively. Time is very valuable, especially if we put it in perspective knowing our days are counted because of a terminal disease. Every minute should count in life. Someday we will have to be held accountable for the way in which we used this valuable thing called time.

Gospel

The gospel is the biggest wealth God has given us to administrate. Although it's free, it doesn't mean it has always been free, but that it cost Jesus' life. It's the only mean of salvation and we are responsible for everything we have and everything we are to fulfill the mission that has been entrusted to us, which is to preach the good news to those who are hopeless.

We could keep on naming things, but I just wanted to share some of them to realize that all of these things come from God and we are just temporary users. Everything lasts as long as our life lasts and one day we will have to come to terms with God; so we have to be wise to enjoy life according to the Father's will. Everything is likely to get lost, worn or break; life, health, etc. In a matter of seconds we can lose it all; that's why we say we are temporary users.

The wisdom of living lies in being good stewards and while we administrate the things God gives us, we can enjoy them. The consequences of not administrating them properly is not being able to enjoy them; we fill ourselves with bitterness, frustration and resentment against the master, and we can't multiply the capital God gave us; as seen in the parable of the talents.

But the benefits of properly administrating are: peace, gratitude, progress, inner healing, security, victory, etc. We don't need to fear the sudden return of the master. However, we need to know the Lord comes and we be held accountable for the things we have done with life and time, abilities and opportunities, work, money and material goods; and above all, what we did with the precious seed of His gospel.

Nothing is ours, but by God's grace we can multiply what we receive, enjoying life as we are faithful stewards to God.

The steward's right attitude

There are two fundamental attitudes: one is faithfulness and responsibility; the other is negligence, unconcern and wickedness, as Jesus tells us about the evil servant in the parable of the talents.

From the moment in which we receive Christ in our lives we have no other option that to assume our role as stewards; but we can choose what kind of steward we will be. The story of Barnabas in Acts 4:36-37 is an example of a faithful steward. Luke registers: *"Joseph, a Levite from Cyprus, whom the apostles called Barnabas (which means "son of encouragement"), sold a field he owned and brought the money and put it at the apostles' feet"*.

The story of Ananias and Sapphira in Acts 5:1-11 is an example of a negligent steward. Luke describes it like this: *"Now a man named Ananias, together with his wife Sapphira, also sold a piece of property. With his wife's full knowledge he kept back part of the money for himself, but brought the rest and put it at the apostles' feet. Then Peter said, 'Ananias, how is it that Satan has so filled your heart that you have lied to the Holy Spirit and have kept for yourself some of the money you received for the land? Didn't it belong to you before it was sold? And after it was sold, wasn't the money at your disposal? What made you think of doing such a thing? You have not lied just to human beings but to God.' When Ananias heard this, he fell down and died. And great fear seized all who heard what had happened. Then some young men came forward, wrapped up his body, and carried him out and buried him. About three hours later his wife came in, not knowing what had happened. Peter asked her, 'Tell me, is this the price you and Ananias got for the land?' 'Yes,' she said, 'that is the price.' Peter said to her, 'How could you conspire to test the Spirit of the Lord? Listen! The feet of the men who buried your husband are at the door, and they will carry you out also'. 'At that moment she fell down at his feet and died. Then the young men came in and, finding her dead, carried her out and buried her beside her husband. Great fear seized the whole church and all who heard about these events".*

Ananias and Sapphira sold their goods, kept a part of what they sold and lied to God and expected to be praised by their brothers for their apparent generosity. That way they were recorded as an example of bad stewards.

The right attitude and motivation of a good steward is:

- **Dependency**. Everything's from God and we completely depend on him. He is who forgives us and trains us to serve him.
- **Consecration**. Paul, in Romans 12:1 says we have to consecrate, surrender, dedicate and commit ourselves. The faithful steward looks after his master's interests, takes care of him and makes him thrive as the faithful servants did in the parable of the talents.
- **Service**. The term 'steward' comes from two Greek words: 'oikos' which means 'house', and 'nomos' which means 'take care, look after'. It always refers to the one who serves; as Joseph did in Potiphar's house, as well as Jesus, who came to serve. Stewardship teaches us that the reason for being Christians is to serve God, His church and our neighbors. Christian who doesn't serve, is useless.
- **Faithfulness and gratitude**. Joseph didn't sin with Potiphar's wife because he understood he couldn't be unfaithful to his master, who had given him so much. The same happens with us Christians, we have to be faithful to God by gratitude until death. In Revelations 2:10, John states: "Do not be afraid of what you are about to suffer. I tell you, the devil will put some of you in prison to test you, and you will suffer persecution for ten days. Be faithful, even to the point of death,

and I will give you life as your victor's crown". He gave us so much: eternal salvation, freed us from eternal condemnation, made us his sons and daughters, gave us a family, gave us gifts and talents and the opportunity of a new life; and above all, he put his trust in us by using us for the extension of His Kingdom. Therefore, gratitude and love have to be the forces that inspire us to serve Him faithfully.

When we obey God with love and gratitude we are happy, and understand that we have nothing outside of His grace and provision. We have no option in being or not being servants; but we can choose to be servants with good attitudes and motivations or not. We don't have to copy the example of Ananias and Sapphira who used God for their own promotion. We do have to copy Joseph and Barnabas who lived lives that honored God because they were faithful under every circumstance.

Stewardship and mission in the Church

Many times we have a very limited idea of stewardship and think that by giving money, for example, we become faithful stewards. But the teaching from the New Testament is clear when telling us that everything belongs to God, including ourselves; and we have to glorify God with our physical lives as well as our spiritual life.

Our mission as a church is to continue Jesus' redeeming work, which basically has two sides: the religious or spiritual one, that is preaching, teaching, and saving; and the social one, that is healing, freeing, feeding, dressing and sheltering. We are God's resource to save with our testimony, with the spiritual gifts the Holy Spirit gives us and with the economic and technical resources we have. The key to fulfill this mission is consecration and commitment.

God Expect and wants us to be faithful and completely con-secrated stewards in life, time, human and spiritual abilities, eco-nomic resources, family, etc. That consecration has to condition our whole life, has to be our priority, as Jesus declares in Matthew 6:33 by saying: *"But seek first His Kingdom and His righteousness, and all these things will be given to you as well"*. Christ must be the founda-tion and the center and His work must be our priority.

This consecration doesn't have to make us neglect the stewardship over our body, but we have to take some time for res-ting, recreating and other things. We must not forget about family and be careful not to make it an escape to not fulfill our responsi-bilities in society.

This consecration does imply that all we do we will do it with quality and faithfulness in the use of time, money and abili-ties. We must manage everything thinking in extending His King-dom, as we commit when we pray the Lord's Prayer.

Facing the fact that Christ gave everything to save us, and make possible the human redemption, this question comes up: How much do we need to give? Each should answer honestly. If we are honest, we should conclude that if we can give more than the 10, 12 or 15%, we should do so. The 10% established by the Old Testament is only a baseline. We have to give everything we own ourselves thinking not only in local necessities but national and worldwide, like missionary works.

We are here to continue Christ's work. He is our example. God wasn't stingy with his Son, Jesus wasn't stingy with his life, what about us? Millions of people are lost and partly it's our res-ponsibility. That is our mission, and stewardship teaches we have to get rid of everything we are and everything we have to reach them with the gospel.

When the disciples untied the donkey for Jesus to get on, in his triumphal entry to Jerusalem, they told the owner: "The Lord needs it" and he said nothing else. Facing that challenge, facing what was done by Christ, and facing the privilege of cooperating with God, let us determine to be faithful stewards since everything belongs to God and we are simple temporary users. Let us have the right attitude and motivation because in the end the master will say: "Well done, good and faithful servant! You have been faithful with a few things; I will put you in charge of many things. Come and share your master's happiness". Let us think about this simple idea that "the Lord needs it" and let us be generous.

Pray: *"Father, give me the ability to discern and understand your necessities through other people. You well said that when we give a glass of water to a thirsty one in your name, or if we visit someone in jail, or dress someone; it's like we did it for you. Let me understand this principle and practice it".*

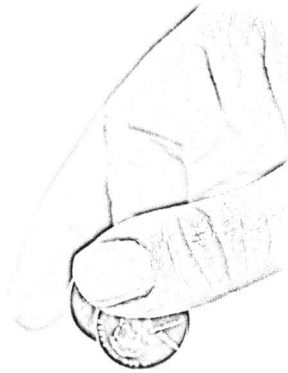

4 – INVESTOR CITIZENS OF THE KINGDOM

There's a tale that tells the story of a pig and a chicken who were walking together through the streets of the city, when suddenly a prestigious fast food restaurant's ad caught their eyes, this said: *"Have scrambled eggs and ham for breakfast today and with the amount of your consumption you will be helping charities"*.

"Well, well", said the chicken to her partner, "So we also have something to do with the charity campaign", to which the pig answered: "Yes, but the difference is that they only ask for your contribution, whilst for me it means sacrifice". How can you qualify what you offer up for Christ's cause? Is it a sacrifice or a mere contribution? There is a very remarkable passage in the Old Testament in reference to this subject of stewardship or administration with the Kingdom's mentality. The author of 1 Chronicles 29:1-18 says the following:

"Then King David said to the whole assembly:

"My son Solomon, the one whom God has chosen, is young and inexperienced. The task is great, because this palatial structure is not for man but for the LORD God. With all my resources I have provided for the temple of my God—gold for the gold work, silver for the silver, bronze for the bronze, iron for the iron and wood for the wood, as well as onyx for the settings, turquoise, stones of various colors, and all kinds of fine stone and marble—all of these in large quantities. Besides, in my devotion to the temple of my God I now give my personal treasures of gold and silver for the temple of my God, over and above everything I have provided for this holy temple: three thousand talents of gold (gold of Ophir) and seven thousand talents of refined silver, for the overlaying of the walls of the buildings, for the gold work and the silver work, and for all the work to be done by the craftsmen. Now, who is willing to consecrate themselves to the LORD today?" Then the leaders of families, the officers of the tribes of Israel, the commanders of thousands and commanders of hundreds, and the officials in charge of the king's work gave willingly. They gave toward the work on the temple of God five thousand talents and ten thousand darics of gold, ten thousand talents of silver, eighteen thousand talents of bronze and a hundred thousand talents of iron. Anyone who had precious stones gave them to the treasury of the temple of the LORD in the custody of Jehiel the Gershonite. The people rejoiced at the willing response of their leaders, for they had given freely and wholeheartedly to the LORD. David the king also rejoiced greatly. David praised the LORD in the

presence of the whole assembly, saying, "Praise be to you, LORD, the God of our father Israel, from everlasting to everlasting. Yours, LORD, is the greatness and the power and the glory and the majesty and the splendor, for everything in heaven and earth is yours. Yours, LORD, is the kingdom; you are exalted as head over all. Wealth and honor come from you; you are the ruler of all things. In your hands are strength and power to exalt and give strength to all. Now, our God, we give you thanks, and praise your glorious name. But who am I, and who are my people, that we should be able to give as generously as this? Everything comes from you, and we have given you only what comes from your hand. We are foreigners and strangers in your sight, as were all our ancestors. Our days on earth are like a shadow, without hope. LORD our God, all this abundance that we have provided for building you a temple for your Holy Name comes from your hand, and all of it belongs to you. I know, my God, that you test the heart and are pleased with integrity. All these things I have given willingly and with honest intent. And now I have seen with joy how willingly your people who are here have given to you. LORD, the God of our fathers Abraham, Isaac and Israel, keep these desires and thoughts in the hearts of your people forever, and keep their hearts loyal to you".

It's important to clarify that the special offerings and normal offerings are different. In this chapter I want to focus on 1 Corinthians passage where Paul the Apostle writes to his church about the subject of offerings. We must remember that the gentile churches of Achaia and Macedone were raising a special offering for the Jewish church of Jerusalem (Acts 11:27-30). This offering would help many Christians in Judea. I want to expand on twelve principles we can apply on the subject of offerings.

It must be regular

In 1 Corinthians 16:2 Paul says: *"On the first day of every week, each one of you should set aside a sum of money in keeping with your income, saving it up, so that when I come, no collections will have to be made"*. The text is clear, it has to be the first day of the week and it has to be a regular practice in Christians. Those who aren't Christians don't have the responsibility of offering, conversely, those who claim to be Christian do; as it's a privilege to be able to do it; it is part of his worship to God, even when the purpose of the money, as in this case, is to meet the temporary necessities of another place.

There are many Christians who give offerings only when their opinions prevail over those of others' or they agree with the purpose and do not realize it's God who we are giving offerings to and we must always do so.

It must be personal

Each and every one of us has the privilege and responsibility of offering. This allows the Christian to give God a part of what he achieved with his work. In the case of people who don't have an income they can give from the resources they receive for personal expenses.

It must be proportional

Everyone has to give proportionally to how they have been

prospered. This has to be with percentages and amounts. Those who earn more should give a bigger percentage than those who earn less. Prosperity should make us more generous and that will show if it's a blessing from God or not.

It must be the reflection of our congregation

The Macedonians were poor people, they were going through difficult situations, but they asked to be allowed to give offerings. Paul, in 2 Corinthians 8:1-5 registers the following: *"And now, brothers and sisters, we want you to know about the grace that God has given the Macedonian churches. In the midst of a very severe trial, their overflowing joy and their extreme poverty welled up in rich generosity. For I testify that they gave as much as they were able, and even beyond their ability. Entirely on their own, they urgently pleaded with us for the privilege of sharing in this service to the Lord's people. And they exceeded our expectations: They gave themselves first of all to the Lord, and then by the will of God also to us"*. The fact that a person is poor doesn't mean he doesn't have the privilege of giving offerings, but according to his possibilities, as the poor widow.

One time, a worker retired, receiving from his partners a photo and a moderate sum of money, product of a collection among themselves. The following day, this worker gave all this money to the church for the missionary work. The pastor suggested him to keep a part of that money to meet his needs of tomorrow. "No pastor", answered the worker, "this money is the result of the Christian testimony that by God's grace I've received from my colleagues and in proof of my gratitude with the Lord I consecrate it to him; and as for tomorrow, I know that who took care of me yesterday will continue to do so tomorrow because he is faithful".

Both this man and the Macedonians gave more than was expected because they had first given themselves to God. What really determines the quality and quantity of a nice offering for God is our consecration. In Luke 21:1-4 Jesus tells the story of the poor widow, saying: *"As Jesus looked up, he saw the rich putting their gifts into the temple treasury. He also saw a poor widow put in two very small copper coins. "Truly I tell you," he said, "this poor widow has put in more than all the others. All these people gave their gifts out of their wealth; but she out of her poverty put in all she had to live on".* She didn't give much, but it was more than what the rich gave because she gave everything she had, whilst the rich gave much but actually took from what they had left over. It was a contribution like in the pig and the chicken's tale.

It must be voluntary and not by obligation

Paul, in 2 Corinthians 8:8-10 states: *"I am not commanding you, but I want to test the sincerity of your love by comparing it with the earnestness of others. For you know the grace of our Lord Jesus Christ, that though he was rich, yet for your sake he became poor, so that you through his poverty might become rich. And here is my judgment about what is best for you in this matter. Last year you were the first not only to give but also to have the desire to do so".* The person must want to give offerings. The offering must be the intern exteriorized desire to give God a part of what you received from Him. Not only should we desire to do so, but it has to be done with the proper motivation of pleasing God. It should be given as a result of emotional conditionings not circumstantial pressures, as Paul registers in 2 Corinthians 9:5 by saying: *"So I thought it necessary to urge the brothers to visit you in advance and finish the arrangements for the generous gift you had promised. Then it will be ready as a generous gift, not as one grudgingly given".*

Offerings must be given for love, expressing generosity and not by anyone's demand. Any offering should be paid as a monthly fee as in neighborhood clubs or charities. Everyone must give voluntarily, generously and freely. Interestingly, another possible translation of the used Greek word generous offering, can be translated as offering of blessing. In other words, Paul is saying that it is possible that some offerings given with wrong motivations can be a curse for the church.

It mustn't suffer necessities.

In 2 Corinthians 9:13-15, Paul establishes that: "*Because of the service by which you have proved yourselves, others will praise God for the obedience that accompanies your confession of the gospel of Christ, and for your generosity in sharing with them and with everyone else. And in their prayers for you their hearts will go out to you, because of the surpassing grace God has given you. Thanks be to God for his indescribable gift!*" God doesn't ask for what we don't have. It's an offense when the church extorts people to give offerings. The church must take care of its poor people. The one who has must give to help the one who doesn't have and this one can't be demanded to give what he doesn't have.

It must be done secretly

In Matthew 6:3-4 Jesus states: "*But when you give to the needy, do not let your left hand know what your right hand is doing, so that your giving may be in secret. Then your Father, who sees what is done in secret, will reward you*". There are many people who have given generously to God but have also ensured that others knew about it. If so, they have already been rewarded with people's praise, but not God's. Our right side mustn't know what our left side does. For example, it's very common in churches that brothers are willing to gift a door or a window for the building, but not to anonymously give the value of that door or window so that later the management team has that money available. At the bottom, there's a necessity in human beings to be seen.

It must be done generously

In 2 Corinthians 9:6-11 Paul says: *"Remember this: Whoever sows sparingly will also reap sparingly, and whoever sows generously will also reap generously. Each of you should give what you have decided in your heart to give, not reluctantly or under compulsion, for God loves a cheerful giver. And God is able to bless you abundantly, so that in all things at all times, having all that you need, you will abound in every good work. As it is written: "They have freely scattered their gifts to the poor; their righteousness endures forever." Now he who supplies seed to the sower and bread for food will also supply and increase your store of seed and will enlarge the harvest of your righteousness. You will be enriched in every way so that you can be generous on every occasion, and through us your generosity will result in thanksgiving to God".*

Who gives, generously prospers. Who has and gives acts like a good steward and the Lord will give him more to invest in His work. According the parable of the talents in Matthew 25:14-30 those who worked and multiplied their master's resources received more to administrate. In verse 28 Jesus says: *"So take the bag of gold from him and give it to the one who has ten bags".*

The motivation is not I GIVE to HAVE MORE, but I GIVE for God's work and I will continue giving to the extent that God trusts me in the stewardship of HIS money. He who is stingy and sows little, will harvest to that extent, especially in joy and life's enjoyment. If I'm stingy with something that's not mine, how can

I pretend to be trusted with more resources?

He who is stingy could have more things, but won't have God's blessing, because he is not administrating everything He gave him for His cause. God has the power to prosper and he wishes that our prosperity will be used to help the needed and for the extension of His Kingdom. The Word declares that God's blessing doesn't bring pain, but wealth.

It must be cheerful

In 2 Corinthians 9:7 Paul states: *"Each of you should give what you have decided in your heart to give, not reluctantly or under compulsion, for God loves a cheerful giver"*. Each of us is responsible in front of God for what we give. There's an old saying that reads: "If it hurts to give, you must give until it stops hurting", which is not biblical nor true. Our offerings must be a joyful expression of gratitude, an offering of ourselves that expresses through money that is an inverted life. The gratitude and appreciation of the blessings make us humble and happy to give. God loves a cheerful giver, because his attitude of life is correct.

It must supply the church's needs

In 2 Corinthians 9:12 Paul states: *"This service that you perform is not only supplying the needs of the Lord's people but is also overflowing in many expressions of thanks to God"*. This passage is placed in a context of famine that came over Judea that therefore affected the church. Our offerings supply the needs of the church so that it can fulfill its mission, and the more we give, more resources there will be to carry out God's will.

There are Christians and churches who think that if they

don't have a pastor they don't have the obligation to give generously, and this reflects a very short vision of the church's mission.
If there's money in excess, locally, nationally or worldwide, there
are always needs we can supply.

It must glorify God

In 2 Corinthians 9:11 and 13 Paul says: *"You will be enriched in
every way so that you can be generous on every occasion, and through
us your generosity will result in thanksgiving to God. Because of the
service by which you have proved yourselves, others will praise God
for the obedience that accompanies your confession of the gospel of
Christ, and for your generosity in sharing with them and with everyone else".* A generous offering and a correct motivation glorifies
God because those who are helped are blessed and therefore are
thankful and praise God. They also do so with saved people. In Philippians 4:10, 14-18, Paul states: "I rejoiced greatly in the Lord that
at last you renewed your concern for me. Indeed, you were con-
cerned, but you had no opportunity to show it. Yet it was good of
you to share in my troubles. Moreover, as you Philippians know,
in the early days of your acquaintance with the gospel, when I
set out from Macedonia, not one church shared with me in the
matter of giving and receiving, except you only; for even when I
was in Thessalonica, you sent me aid more than once when I was
in need. Not that I desire your gifts; what I desire is that more be
credited to your account. I have received full payment and have
more than enough. I am amply supplied, now that I have received
from Epaphroditus the gifts you sent. They are a fragrant offering,
an acceptable sacrifice, pleasing to God". How people enjoy when
the church helps them in their pain and need! How they thank
God! Let us be partakers of that joy, let us be directly involved and
not merely spectators.

It must be an example of love and obedience

In 2 Corinthians 9:13 Paul clarifies: *"Because of the service by which you have proved yourselves, others will praise God for the obedience that accompanies your confession of the gospel of Christ, and for your generosity in sharing with them and with everyone else"*. Jesus is the great example. For love, He humbled Himself, as Paul establishes in Philippians 2:5-8 by saying: *"In your relationships with one another, have the same mindset as Christ Jesus: Who, being in very nature God, did not consider equality with God something to be used to his own advantage; rather, he made himself nothing by taking the very nature of a servant, being made in human likeness. And being found in appearance as a man, he humbled himself by becoming obedient to death— even death on a cross!"* Jesus obeyed in everything to make our salvation possible.

When we give we are an example of love for God and those who need Christ and our help. But we are also an example of obedience. As stewards we are fulfilling our responsibility to manage God's goods. Offerings measure our level of consecration, faithfulness, love and obedience to God. Offerings glorify God, since it's our privilege and responsibility. In 1 Corinthians 6:19-20 Paul asks: *"Do you not know that your bodies are temples of the Holy Spirit, who is in you, whom you have received from God? You are not your own; you were bought at a price. Therefore honor God with your bodies"*.

The apostle Paul wasn't talking about quantities, but about consecration, gratitude and responsibility. May the Father give us grace and wisdom to manage His economic resources with these and other principles and give glory to His name.

A story tells that in a church a man, who used to waste all

his money gambling, converts. Upon entering the baptistery the day of his baptism, a friend tells him: "Hey man, your wallet's in your pocket, it's going to get wet". And he answered: "I left on purpose because I want it to be baptized with me". The question for us would be if our wallet has been converted and baptized with us.

Pray: *"Dear God and Father, I desire with all my heart that you make me generous towards you and your work and let my offerings be more than a collaboration. Amen".*

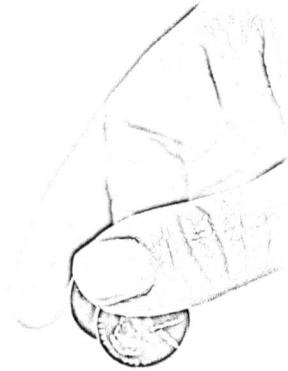

5 - CITIZENS WITH A MISSION IN THE KINGDOM

In this chapter I would like to share some general steward-ship principles to understand why we are stewards and how we should develop such responsibility in a way it pleases the King. In previous chapters I talked about the basic concepts that qualify us as stewards of the King. I haven't focused much on how to proceed; in fact, I wanted us to know that we have to be like God's stewards.

When we understand what we are in relation to all these things, when we know how the correct attitude should be like and which are our priorities as stewards, we don't have the need to be told what to do, nor how much we have to give. Yes, we have to be trained and we also need to get organized, but our attitude, our disposition and our consecration will allow God to work in us, through us and even through the things we give in consecration.

However, many may wonder, should we or should we not tithe? Is the teaching of tithing in the Old or the New Testament?

This takes us to consider three things in this chapter. I'd like us to remember the passage in Matthew 25:14-30 where Jesus says:

> *"Again, it will be like a man going on a journey, who called his servants and entrusted his wealth to them. To one he gave five bags of gold, to another two bags, and to another one bag, each according to his ability. Then he went on his journey. The man who had received five bags of gold went at once and put his money to work and gained five bags more. So also, the one with two bags of gold gained two more. But the man who had received one bag went off, dug a hole in the ground and hid his master's money. After a long time the master of those servants returned and settled accounts with them. The man who had received five bags of gold brought the other five. 'Master,' he said, 'you entrusted me with five bags of gold. See, I have gained five more.' "His master replied, 'Well done, good and faithful servant! You have been faithful with a few things; I will put you in charge of many things. Come and share your master's happiness!' The man with two bags of gold also came. 'Master,' he said, 'you entrusted me with two bags of gold; see, I have gained two more.' His master replied, 'Well done, good and faithful servant! You have been faithful with a few things; I will put you in charge of many things. Come and share your master's happiness!' Then the man who had received one bag of gold came. 'Master,' he said, 'I knew that you are a hard man, harvesting where you have not sown and gathering where you have not scattered seed. So I was afraid and went out and hid your gold in the ground. See, here is what be-*

longs to you.' His master replied, 'You wicked, lazy servant! So you knew that I harvest where I have not sown and gather where I have not scattered seed? Well then, you should have put my money on deposit with the bankers, so that when I returned I would have received it back with interest. 'So take the bag of gold from him and give it to the one who has ten bags. For whoever has will be given more, and they will have an abundance. Whoever does not have, even what they have will be taken from them. And throw that worthless servant outside, into the darkness, where there will be weeping and gnashing of teeth".

What is complete stewardship?

This question has three basic answers:

Everything belongs to God. This means God is the owners of everything, not only a percentage like 5, 10 or 15%. He is the owner of absolutely everything.

- We are not our own. In 1 Corinthians 6:19-20 Paul asks: "Do you not know that your bodies are temples of the Holy Spirit, who is in you, whom you have received from God? You are not your own; you were bought at a price. Therefore honor God with your bodies". If I am not mine, then everything I do belongs to the owner. I receive a part as an income that allows me to live by meeting my needs. Everything we get in life, whether it's the family, career, financial resources, work, influences, etc. is God's, not ours.
- God made us stewards. When the Bible says we are stewards, it means in a complete way. We are not only stewards

of the money, but of everything we are and have. We must use everything and enjoy with attitude of service towards Him. That's why the proper question to ask ourselves is: "What is my part? And, what part belongs to God? This takes us to consider the second important point:

Why should I give to God?

If God doesn't need anything, why should I give him if I need more than He does? God needs nothing for him, but he needs people and things to carry out His mission of saving humanity; He needs things to bless His children and to save the lost. He doesn't need those who believe themselves indispensable. God's Kingdom will continue to expand even when those indispensable people die.

This takes us to think that God's mission is worldwide and goes much further than our human perspective. Jesus said, in Acts 1:8: *"But you will receive power when the Holy Spirit comes on you; and you will be my witnesses in Jerusalem, and in all Judea and Samaria, and to the ends of the earth"*. And to accomplish this commandment, to get the resources God has given us, it implies the whole church getting involved.

We must not only think of local needs, but the whole world's needs. We must not only think of the needs of our organization, but develop a Kingdom mentality. As a family, we have been blessed many times by people and churches outside the congregations in which we have been serving and outside the organization in which we have been involved. We have been direct beneficiaries of this Kingdom mentality.

Our task is not only with a small part of the church or our area, but with all mankind. Facing this proposal we can see that the demands are very high and we have to get involved. This takes us to the third point to consider:

What Does God need to fulfill his mission?

Money. This is a very clear need since without financial resources we can't address works, such as:

- Buildings and facilities. We can't build, repair, paint, maintain, pay services, etc.
- Ministries. To develop them we need financial resources to pay expenses for evangelistic campaigns, pay salaries, buy discipleship material, produce study materials, get involved with missions or community service.
- Administration. We need financial resources to get items for the office, computers, projectors, boards, etc. There are many jobs that require financial resources. When we think of our offerings we have to keep in mind God's complete work.

The gospels and apostolic letters do not talk about tithe because in Jesus' mentality, and therefore the disciples' mentality, it wasn't that the law of tithe was obsolete, but Jesus went a step further. He declared that if our justice didn't surpass that of the scribes and Pharisees then we hadn't understood his message. When you understand that everything belongs to God and that He trusts me that I will get involves in His Kingdom, He leaves in me the responsibility of how much I want to invest as a good steward. From that perspective, God expects you to invest more than the 10%.

The apostolic letters talk about meeting needs. The primitive church gave offerings with that purpose. In Acts we read that there were brothers who sold their properties and gave the total of what was sold so that the apostles would administrate it in the extension of the Kingdom and to meet the needs of those who needed something to eat. Today our chapel is the world, and therefore if God gives us resources, we must get involved in God's worldwide work.

The problem that lies, many time, in Christians is that we give only to supply local needs and we don't have a complete sense of stewardship or a Kingdom mentality. If we can give more than the 10, 15 or 20% and we don't give it, it means we are not good stewards. But, besides money, we need:

People. Paul, in Ephesians 4:11-13 says: *"So Christ himself gave the apostles, the prophets, the evangelists, the pastors and teachers, to equip his people for works of service, so that the body of Christ may be built up until we all reach unity in the faith and in the know-ledge of the Son of God and become mature, attaining to the whole measure of the fullness of Christ"*. God needs people to fulfill his complete work, such as:

- Ministries. Teachings, preaching, evangelism, counseling, worship, visitation, etc.
- Service. Administration, maintenance, social work, cleaning, etc.

God needs redeemed people, people who don't believe themselves indispensable or the last coke in the desert. This people constitute the body of Christ, through whom He continues his work. He doesn't send angels, because they weren't saved. We have been saved and rescued by God and we can be an example of the power of his gospel. Paul states in 2 Corinthians 5:18-20 that it was God who gave us the ministry of reconciliation by saying: *"All this is from God, who reconciled us to himself through Christ and gave us the ministry of reconciliation: that God was reconciling the world to himself in Christ, not counting people's sins against them. And he has committed to us the message of reconciliation. We are therefore Christ's ambassadors, as though God was exhorting them through us. We implore you on Christ's behalf: Be reconciled to God".*

How much of ourselves do we need to give? We need to give the necessary time to be trained, the necessary time to use the gifts and talents he gave us in an effective service. We have to provide the necessary time to have a life of proper relationship with God through a personal time of intimacy with him. We have to give the necessary time to glorify God with our body and spirit. Giving myself to God must not affect the stewardship of my body or family. I have to dedicate time to be with and enjoy my family.

A good steward will do everything thinking in the Lord, as Paul establishes in Colossians 3:17, 23-24: "And whatever you do, whether in word or deed, do it all in the name of the Lord Jesus, giving thanks to God the Father through him. Whatever you do, work at it with all your heart, as working for the Lord, not for human masters, since you know that you will receive an inheritance from the Lord as a reward. It is the Lord Christ you are serving". You will also be thinking in His work and will be pleasing God and He will honor and provide you at all times.

According to the introductory passage in Matthew 25, we have to be good stewards. Verse 19 tells us He will come. The Lord won't take long. Let's wait for him workings like good and faithful stewards.

Pray: *"Lord, I want to give you all you have lent me and everything I am by your grace, because everything is yours and from thy hand I give. Amen".*

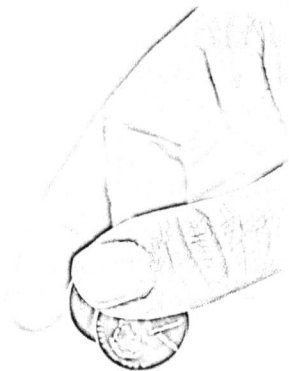

6 - WHEN THE **LAW** OF TITHE STEALS THE **GRACE** OF GENEROSITY
- part 1 -

In the last few years of our pastoral ministry we have asked our congregations: If the concept of tithing disappeared, would you give God less, more or the same? What's surprising about this survey is that almost everyone agreed they would give the same or more.

Why am I going to address this issue? Actually, when I understood this issue, my idea was to publish a book exclusively a-ddressing to the subject and this title, but I understood that I could hurt susceptibilities, so I preferred to include two chapters in other subjects and provide a wider view, that is the actual pro-posal. A few incidents encouraged me to address this issue and I want to do with fear of not offending anyone.

- Months of prayer and meditation on it. Besides a deep con-versation with Paula (my wife), which started one day in our car and then was continued at home.

- Someone´s thoughts about the time given for the offerings in one of the churches we pastored. This person shared a concept expressing that many times he gave offerings by obligation.
- A brother's prayer for the moment of the offerings. In one of his prayer's lines he told God that if there was any brother or sister there who didn't have what to give as an offering that he/she should borrow God.
- A check I saw at the house of a church's reviser that represented a sister's tithe. The amount was $268,70. I wondered why it had to be so precise.
- A few conversations I've had about this subject with a good friend and brother in the gospel, Mauricio. A generous man in his giving to the Kingdom. He was a member of our church and now lives in Spain.
- A letter I received on one of my birthdays, from someone I love. Further on you will be able to read it. This letter was the trigger for me to start not only to live this principle but also to teach it.

The apostle Paul, writing to the Corinthians states: *"Remember this: Whoever sows sparingly will also reap sparingly, and whoever sows generously will also reap generously. Each of you should give what you have decided in your heart to give, not reluctantly or under compulsion, for God loves a cheerful giver. And God is able to bless you abundantly, so that in all things at all times, having all that you need, you will abound in every good work. As it is written: They have freely scattered their gifts to the poor; their righteousness endures forever."*

Now he who supplies seed to the sower and bread for food will also supply and increase your store of seed and will enlarge the harvest of your righteousness. You will be enriched in every way so that you can be generous on every occasion, and through us your generosity will result in thanksgiving to God. (2 Corinthians 9:6-11)

The first thing that stands out from this passage is generosity. But I want us to focus on a very important aspect before. If we understand this revelation, the rest will be easy to assimilate. When we read the Bible and look at our own lives, we realize that in many areas there's a progressive growth. Notice for example:

Progressive education. If your grandparents didn't finish elementary school, your parents didn't finish high school; it's expected from you to finish university.

Progressive prosperity. God never opposed to prosperity, but He sees it as a progressive prosperity from generation to generation. He doesn't come to take away anything from us, on the contrary, he comes to add. All those who reached for God received promises of lands. It's the human being who today wants to get rich quickly and in any way. I went to school barefoot, especially on rainy and cold days, because I assisted a rural school. Having only one pair of shoes, on rainy days I went barefoot, got to school, washed my feet in a puddle and then put on my shoes. That way I could have my feet dry during the four hours of class. But today I wouldn't let my children do the same because they don't have the need to do it. I don't believe in the gospel of prosperity, but I do believe that the gospel will prosper you.

Progressive responsibility. When our kids are young we give them 1$ for their expenses, as they grow, we give them 2$, then 5$, then 10$ and so on, until they learn to administrate bigger amounts. Today our oldest daughter has a job and manages her own money.

Progressive baptism. First John's baptism, that of repentance, later Jesus' as a sign that we are his children, and lastly the Holy Spirit's, which enables us with power for the Kingdom. Paul even talks about the baptism of suffering in the letter to the Philippians.

Progressive revelation. First we have an awareness of God's existence, then we learn a little about the Bible: faith, Jesus, the Holy Spirit, etc. and as years go by, God reveals the secrets of his person. Growing up in the countryside and not having electric lights, I did my school homework with my brothers, under the light of a kerosene lamp. Now my nephews can do the same but with electric lights. It would be improper for my brother to pretend his sons to go back 30 years. The same happens on a spiritual level. Many Christian doctrines or practices from a few years ago reflect a certain amount of light or revelation. But as this is progressive, there are now doctrines and practices we see in a different way. That doesn't mean our parents or grandparents were wrong, they acted and were faithful to the light they had received. But today we have more light and therefore a bigger responsibility before God.

Progressive theology. The New Testament is a more finished theology, more complete than the Old Testament. For example:

- In Genesis we see how God gave man His Spirit, but in the New Testament we see how God gave us His Son.
- We see that the cost God paid in the New Testament exceeds the cost He paid in the Genesis. In previous chapters I shared this anecdote; that is nice to remember here again: On the window of a restaurant there was an ad that said: "Today we have ham and scrambled eggs". Then in smaller words said: "A percentage of the proceeds will be given to the missions". In front of the restaurant a pig and a chicken were talking. The happy chicken says: "We also participate in this people's

missionary project!" The pig angrily answers: "Yes, I saw it, but it's not fair because it only costs you an egg, but it costs my life". In the Old Testament the forgiveness of sins was obtained by the death of a lamb. In the New Testament, to obtain complete and definitive forgiveness God has to give His own Son's life.

- In Exodus God gave his children manna, but in the New Testament God gives us the Bread of Life, that is the life of His Son Jesus Christ.
- In Exodus God gave the Israelites two tablets of the covenant law. In Acts God gave His sons (the church) the Holy Spirit.

Similarly we note there's a progressive growth in our offerings to God. We started with a context of alms, we move on a little more and someone talks about tithing, but many Christians stay there.

The subject "When the LAW of tithing steals the GRACE of generosity" is central to this book. I want us to see that although tithing is something biblical I don't believe it's for Christians to cling on to it forever. The tithes were a part of God's program for the period of law. We will see how the law of tithing was the tutor to teach us to be generous, to take us to a financial liberality and freedom. Our justice must be bigger than that of the scribes and Pharisees".

The evangelical church has slaved Christians with tithing and has stolen the grace of generosity. We have done something that once was an effective tool of slavery and subjugation for these days.

Someone may refute that Jesus didn't come to abolish the law but to enforce it. It's true that this is how it is, but it's good to remember that he says it in a context to reaffirm the Ten Commandments and not in a context of tithe. Note these details:

- In the Old Testament there were lamb sacrifices, but not anymore in the New Testament, because Christ is the perfect lamb.
- In the Old Testament children were circumcised, but not anymore in the New Testament. Now we talk about a heart circumcision.
- In the Old Testament worship to God was centralized in the temple of Jerusalem, but not anymore in the New Testament, now we are the temple of God and we can worship Him wherever we are.
- In the Old Testament God's word was written on stone tablets, but in the New Testament it is written on our hearts of flesh.

Now, an interesting question arises: why do we continue with tithing in this period? If we read the New Testament we don't find any passage that talks about tithing as something current. The two favorite passages that are never mentioned are: One when Jesus says reproachfully to the religious leaders that they gave offerings and tithes from mint and cumin, but they forgot about mercy. Then he says that it was okay to do the first but not to forget the second. We need to remind ourselves that we were still in the period of the law, because the period of grace begins after Jesus' resurrection and especially after the Pentecost, with the Holy Spirit's arrival.

The other favorite passage of the ones who stand for tithing is when the author of the Hebrews in chapter 7 says, *"Abraham gave Melchizedek a tenth of everything"*. It's also good to remember a hermeneutics principle that is to read the whole context of the phrase. By doing so we discover that the subject addressed in this chapter is not tithing but that the author uses it to argue that Jesus' priesthood is superior to that of Melchizedek, Moses or Aaron.

In the extent in which the author of this letter develops his argument he says the following in Hebrews 7:12: *"For when the priesthood is changed, the law must be changed also"*. Abel and Cain offered offerings. Noah offered offerings, then Abraham, Moses, David, etc. up to Malachi, all of them offered offerings and tithes. But it's essential to note that the lineage of Levi's priesthood from the Old Testament was replaced by a new lineage, Judah's, where the Messiah comes from, the High priest by excellence.

I want us to observe that for the period of grace, under this new priesthood, God has established a category that exceeds that of tithes, he establishes the category of the "generous offering" that is not centralized in men, but in the Kingdom, which does not always represent a specific percentage, but that grows and can always be different.

Have you ever thought of living with the 10% and giving the 90% for the Kingdom? Instead of asking ourselves "how much should I give God?" we should ask ourselves "how much do I need for living?" Throughout our years of ministry we have met people who were very faithful with tithe, but with a disastrous and egocentric administration of the remaining 90%. We have known churches where tithe represented a 90% of the congregation's incomes and offerings only a 10%. If tithe was a commandment, that is something that corresponds to God, then it would be appropriate to ask ourselves if the congregation is generous in their giving to God. I think the answer is quite obvious. It's a definite NO. It's a miserable, egocentric and stingy congregation. It would be generous if the offering's percentage were closer to that of the tithes in the congregation's general budget.

Note that Paul recommends that no one gives "by obligation nor by necessity". Nowadays we have many things that expire monthly. If we don't pay the electricity bill, the company comes and turns it off. If we don't pay for water, the company comes and turns it off. If don't pay for gas, the company comes and turns it off. If we don't pay for the telephone, the company comes and turns it off. For many years the church has taught that if we don't pay the tithe God turns off his blessings.

Now, if we are tithing because of that, then we are tithing by obligation. And God doesn't want tithe if it's given that way, because your heart is not in him and you do it by fear. That is law, and it causes you sadness. Tithing as a law is another expiration and if you do it, it condemns you.

Paul says to Philemon that *"But I did not want to do a-nything without your consent, so that any favor you do would not seem forced but would be voluntary."* Although he is talking about sending his slave Onesimus back to the master's house, the principle can be applied to the area of our giving. God doesn't want anything from us that is not a voluntary offering.

The church has also taught that if you want 'God to bless you, then you have to give tithes, or what is fashionable now, 'agree with God'. And we forget that the only who has the right to establish pacts is God and we have to accept them or not. Many Christians, instead of gambling at the casino, have made tithing a religious game where they expect to win a lot and receive God's blessing to then stop working.

Now, the Word says that if you do it by necessity, it's also not an offering centered in God, but in you and therefore He's not interested. It's better if you keep your money. Doing it this way is like a transaction and it doesn't bring blessing but curse.

Luke, in the book of Acts wrote the story of Simon the Magician. In Acts 8:17-23 he tells us that as this man saw the power coming from the apostles' hands, he offered them money to have what they had. Luke writes it like this: *"When Simon saw that the Spirit was given at the laying on of the apostles' hands, he offered them money and said, "Give me also this ability so that everyone on whom I lay my hands may receive the Holy Spirit."* (Acts 8:18-19)

Peter answered: *"May your money perish with you, because you thought you could buy the gift of God with money! You have no part or share in this ministry, because your heart is not right before God. Repent of this wickedness and pray to the Lord in the hope that he may forgive you for having such a thought in your heart. For I see that you are full of bitterness and captive to sin".* (Acts 8:20-23)

In the last few years I've heard about and seen very often people who buy their apostle's titles, who buy revelations, or buy a prophetic word. We have to be very careful with this, in case we are in the same position as Simon the Magician and the same fate awaits for us.

As Paul in 1 Corinthians 13 tells us about a better way than the gifts of the Holy Spirit, which is love, in the same way the New Testament teaches us a better way as to giving, that is not tithing, but generous, overflowing, tight offering; that as time goes by should exceed the 10%.

In Galatians 3:23-25 Paul says: *"But before faith came, we were kept under guard by the law, kept for the faith which would afterward be revealed. Therefore the law was our tutor to bring us to Christ, that we might be justified by faith. But after faith has come, we are no longer under a tutor".*

A stake is like a guide we put to a tree for it to grow straight. Once the tree has grown it no longer needs the guide. In the same way, tithing was a stake in the Old Testament, a guide to teach God's people to give for the Kingdom with generosity.

If you still haven't learnt the grace of giving, it's because you are still kept under the guard of the law, you are slaved, and you haven't assumed the responsibility of an adult son or of a Kingdom's citizen.

God's proposal for us is to become generous sons and daughters prepared to give, prepared to invest not only with money, but with time, abilities and talents for the extension of the Kingdom.

As of now, think of this "The size of your offering represents the value you give to what God has given you". "The size of your offering represents your definite commitment to God's work here on earth". The widow gave more than anyone, because what she gave represented her love for God. She gave everything she had although it was the smallest current coin.

God want to bless you, God want to free your economy, but He can't do it if you are under the guidance of the law, of fear, or to giving by necessity. He expects to find his children giving with happiness and generosity, expectant of what God will do. Some years ago God let me visit one of the biggest churches in Guatemala. At the time of the offerings I witnessed something I had never seen before. People ran down the stands, with their o-fferings in hand, screaming from joy because they had the privilege of worshiping God through this act of generosity. And what an act, that church has built buildings with costs of over 10 million dollars with Guatemalan money, in a social and economic context where the average of monthly salaries are around u$s 100.00.

I want to challenge you to learn with me (because I'm still in this unending process of learning) to give generous offerings and to begin to walk this path of freedom God gives us. If we don't believe in the principle of generosity, it's better to withdraw our offerings from the storehouse and invest elsewhere.

Pray: *"Dear Father, take from me any wrong motivation at the moment of my offerings. Search my heart and see if there is a perverse path. Let me always give you with generosity and joy. In your name. Amen".*

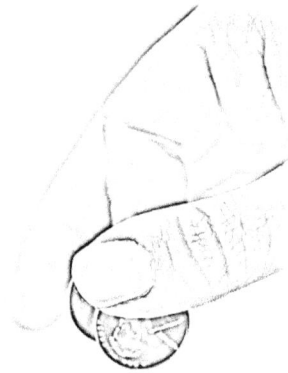

7 - WHEN THE **LAW** OF TITHE STEALS THE **GRACE** OF GENEROSITY
- parte 2 -

I want to refer again the passage in 2 Corinthians 9:6-11 where Paul says the following:

> *"Remember this: Whoever sows sparingly will also reap sparingly, and whoever sows generously will also reap generously. Each of you should give what you have decided in your heart to give, not reluctantly or under compulsion, for God loves a cheerful giver. And God is able to bless you abundantly, so that in all things at all times, having all that you need, you will abound in every good work. As it is written: "They have freely scattered their gifts to the poor; their righteousness endures forever." Now he who supplies seed to the sower and bread for food will also supply and increase your store of seed and will enlarge the harvest of your righteousness. You*

will be enriched in every way so that you can be generous on every occasion, and through us your generosity will result in thanksgiving to God".

This takes us to establish a profile of Kingdom's citizen in our period, the one of the grace, taking into account the following characteristics:

A citizen of the Kingdom is generous, because he understands that his person is not worth for what he has, but for who has him.

In Luke 12:15 Jesus warns us: *"Then he said to them, 'Watch out! Be on your guard against all kinds of greed; life does not consist in an abundance of possessions'".* The world has made us believe that we are worth for what we have, but God tells us we are worth for the fact that He lives in us.

It is said that finding himself in the brink of death, Alexander the Great called his generals and told them his last three wishes:

1. That his coffin was carried on the shoulders and transported by the best doctors of the time.
2. That the treasures he had conquered (silver, gold, gems) were scattered on the road to his grave, and…
3. That his hands remained hanging outside the coffin and at everyone's sight.

One of his generals, surprised by his unusual wishes, asked Alexander what were his reasons.

Alexander explained:

1. I want the best doctors to carry my coffin to show that they DON'T have, facing death, the power to heal.
2. I want the floor to be covered with my treasures so that everyone can see that the material goods conquered here, here remain.
3. I want my hands to swing with the wind, so that people can see we come with empty hands and with empty hands we leave, when our greatest treasure, that is time, ends.

A citizen of the Kingdom is a generous being, because it understands God gave everything for him/her.

1 John 4:10 says: *"This is love: not that we loved God, but that he loved us and sent his Son as an atoning sacrifice for our sins"*. In 2 Corinthians 8:1-2 Paul says: *"And now, brothers and sisters, we want you to know about the grace that God has given the Macedonian churches. In the midst of a very severe trial, their overflowing joy and their extreme poverty welled up in rich generosity"*.

It's good to remember that generosity doesn't depend on how much we earn, but on how much we need to live. We can earn $10000 monthly, but if we spend $9950, then we only have a range of 50$ to be generous.

John 3:16 says: *"For God so loved the world that he gave his one and only Son, that whoever believes in him shall not perish but have eternal life"*. To be generous we need to deny ourselves. And to deny ourselves, we need God's grace.

A citizen of the Kingdom is generous because he battles against greed.

Paul in 2 Corinthians 9:5 says: *"So I thought it necessary to urge the brothers to visit you in advance and finish the arrangements for the generous gift you had promised. Then it will be ready as a generous gift, not as one grudgingly given"*. The size of our offering reveals our high or low greed. Some preacher used to say, at the time of the offerings: "Give until it stops hurting". Although it seems a mistaken concept, it is also true that many times greed plays a trick on us and doesn't allow us to be generous.

A citizen of the Kingdom knows that the grace of generosity is the key to break the law of poverty.

Proverbs 11:25 states: *"A generous person will prosper; whoever refreshes others will be refreshed"*. Do you want to break the cycle of poverty in your life? Start to give. The world says that to become rich you have to save, but God tells you that you have to give generously. But is good to remind ourselves that the prosperity God talks about is not something instantaneous, but a result of a generational process.

A citizen of the Kingdom is generous because he knows it's better to give than to receive.

Acts 20:35 says: *"It is more blessed to give than to receive"* (Boxers' favorite verse). There's an inner satisfaction that happens when we give that is different to what we can feel when we receive something.

A citizen of the Kingdom is generous because he knows life is a boomerang, that if we sow scarcely, we will also harvest scarcely.

Jesus in Luke 6:38 says: *"Give, and it will be given to you.*

A good measure, pressed down, shaken together and running over, will be poured into your lap. For with the measure you use, it will be measured to you". Paul in 2 Corinthians 9:6 states: *"Remember this: Whoever sows sparingly will also reap sparingly, and whoever sows generously will also reap generously"*. There are spiritual principles that are universal, like the law of gravity. No matter how consecrated we are, if we jump from an eighth floor, we will probably die. Similarly, regardless if we are Christians or not; if we are generous in our giving, we will receive more seeds to sow.

A citizen of the Kingdom is someone who is constantly learning to be more generous.

Paul said in Timothy: *"Command them to do good, to be rich in good deeds, and to be generous and willing to share"*. I must admit that I'm not as generous as God expects me to be, but I want to keep on learning this spiritual law. As a church we have to talk more about this issue. Jesus talked more about money than about heaven. Sometimes we think that if we talk too much about the subject we can deviate from the centrality of the gospel; but it's good to remind ourselves what Jesus used to say to the people in his times, for example that "we can't serve two lords, we can't serve God and mammon (god of greed)".

A citizen of the Kingdom works, not only to meet his needs, but also to give with generosity for the extension of the Kingdom.

You may say you can't give because you don't have a job. Pray, ask God to give a job that allows you to meet your needs and be generous with Him and His Kingdom and you will see God will open the doors. There's a principle we can apply in everything we have or want to have. For example, if you are thinking on buying or building a house, do it so that you have a space to shelter someone in need. If you are thinking on buying a car, think of one that not only meets your needs but that allows you to take someone in need.

A citizen of the Kingdom knows there are people, like the widow, the indigent or the orphan, who needs the church to help them and not to take their last pennies.

Therefore be generous when giving, so the church can carry out this work with the needy. If you want to help someone in particular that's related to the church, try doing so through the church, that way you won't be building a reputation for your name, but you will have Jesus magnified through the church. You will also avoid future problems.

A citizen of the Kingdom is generous because he knows his generosity is intimately linked to God's generosity.

Our generosity is a reflection of our fullness of the Holy Spirit. In other words, a greedy person is not full of the Holy Spirit. The fuller we are of the Holy Spirit, the more generous we will be! Jesus was 100% full of the Holy Spirit, that's why He could give the 100% of his life on our favor.

In Acts 2:44-45 and 4:32 Luke writes:

"All the believers were together and had everything in common. They sold property and possessions to give to anyone who had need". "All the believers were one in heart and mind. No one claimed that any of their possessions was their own, but they

shared everything they had".

As a church we should open an office to receive property titles. Why were they so generous? Simply because they were full of, baptized by, and submerged in the Holy Spirit and they understood that what they had received from God was so big that they showed it with their extreme generosity. They broke the 10% cycle from the Old Testament and submerged into the New Testament's new proposal of generosity.

A citizen of the Kingdom doesn't focus his life on giving, but on receiving from the Holy Spirit.

Giving is an equitable answer to what we have received. Our offering is the value we give to what God gave us. If we think that what we receive from God is worth $5, then that is what we will give. But if we are convinced that what He gave us is priceless, then we will always be willing to give with generosity not only our money but also talents, gifts and time.

A citizen of the Kingdom understands God works by stations.

There's a time to give and a time to receive, there's a time to sow and a time to harvest, as Ecclesiastes 3:1-8 says. That means that in practice there can be weeks in which we cannot give God much, but there can be others in which we can give much more than the 10, 12 or 20%. We live in a society marked by the salary that in many countries is monthly or biweekly and sometimes weekly. If we receive a monthly salary, most logically and probably is that in the first week, after collecting, our amount of generosity will be different than weeks after.

A citizen of the Kingdom is generous with God's work because he know that the most practical way of expressing he is committed to God's project is through His church.

In other words, if you are not convinced that your pastors and leaders are doing a great work for God, then keep your money; but if you are convinced that what they are doing is from God, then be the most generous you can be, giving not by obligation nor necessity, but with conviction and love. Let's observe Nehemiah, when he faced the reconstruction of the walls of Jerusalem, he received a generous help not only from the people of Jerusalem, but also from the Assyrian king. That shows us another principle, that when a project is from God, He will provide the resources through his children or other people or companies.

A citizen of the Kingdom is generous with God's work in general.

That is to say that our generosity is not limited only to the local church, but we can express our generosity with other organizations, institutions and people; but understanding that our main commitment is with the local church. The german preacher, Dietrich Bonhoeffer said: *"What's good and righteous can only emerge from a pacific, free and generous heart. That has been my experience through life"*. Generosity is and evidence of a good and noble heart.

What does all this mean to us? It means that:

1. We should eradicate from our language and practice the concept of tithe.
2. We must get in our minds and hearts the concept of a gene-

rous offering, which many times is bigger that the tithe, because we are growing in giving to God.

3. We should teach this new concept to new people in discipleship programs.

4. We must understand that God doesn't mind percentages, but He sees if our heart is generous or not. For a retired person, 100$ of his pension could mean a lot more than the 500$ of a person who has a good income. Otherwise, let's note the offering of the poor widow. A detail that might have slipped from the story is that this widow didn't give the 10% of her salary, but the 100%. She gave everything.

5. We must share with others what God is doing in us to help us grow. If Paul in 2 Corinthians says that the offering they gathered for the poor was generous, is because they had counted it. Exodus 35 and 36 tells us about Moses, who was gathering offerings for the construction of the sanctuary and at one point had to tell the people to stop bringing offerings. If they came to that point it was because those who were gathering told Moses about the people's generosity. We need to share and listen to testimonies of what God is doing in us in that area, since it's the most practical way of reflecting the truth about this principle.

A few years ago, for my birthday, my wife organized a small party. That day, family, friends and brothers in faith gave me gifts, which I deeply appreciated. But I want to share with you something personal that happened to me that day. When I went to sleep that night, I found under my pillow a letter that read the following:

> *"Dear dad. Happy birthday. God has been good and has given you a nice day. I know you have received*

many gifts today. I would have liked to give you a big present, because you are nice and you deserve it. But I give you this, which is everything I have. With love, Chris..."

As I read I couldn't stop crying. I went to my son's bedroom (he was 8 or 9 years old), he hadn't fell asleep yet so I told him: "Chris, today many people gave me beautiful and valuable gifts, but I want you to know that yours' exceeded all of them". It was AR$ 7 (approximately U$D 1), which could mean nothing for many readers. But it was everything he had.

The following Sunday, being at church I could give God the best gift my son gave me. It wasn't much, but it was the best gift I got.

I want to encourage you to have an opportunity to give a generous offering. Don't give by necessity or obligation. Give by and with love. Be generous with your offering, knowing God gave everything for you with His Son's life and He keeps giving you everything you need to have a full life here and the certainty of an eternal life.

In Exodus 34:20 and Deuteronomy 16:16-17 God reminds us that we shouldn't show up with empty hands and Paul adds to this thought, that we should give according to the way God has prospered us.

Pray: *"God, thank you because you established an equitable principle for everyone, which is to give generously for the extension of your Kingdom. Let me keep growing every day in this area of my life, as I have grown in others. In Jesus' name. Amen"*

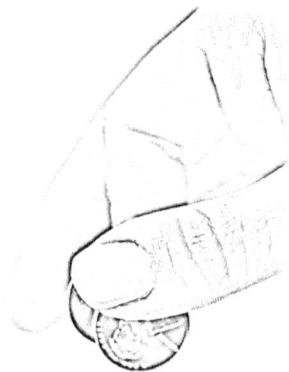

8 - THE TRIPLE UNCTION

After Israel's return from captivity in Babylon, God sends a prophet named Haggai to encourage his people to reconstruct the temple of Jerusalem, which was destroyed as a consequence of the last enemy invasion.

Haggai is a prophet with very little time in the ministry, he is considered as one of the Minor Prophets, not because of the quality in his ministry but because of the brevity, since in terms of quality he has been very rich and transcendent. It´s a book that only contains two chapters. In the first chapter, God makes his people see their negligence in living in very nice houses and palaces, but with a temple, which was the center and central axis of Israel´s life in those times, completely destroyed.

We can apply this on a spiritual and physical level. As for the physical level, we could be neglecting God´s house, the place of meetings, while we live in comfortable places and move around in new cars. But we can also apply it to the spiritual level, while we give bigger transcendence to our exterior life: house, family, work, business, etc. and neglect our interior life: our character, the fruit of the Spirit, spiritual disciplines, etc.

But actually this chapter is based on the first 9 verses in chapter 2. The text says the following:

> *"On the twenty-first day of the seventh month, the word of the LORD came through the prophet Haggai: 'Speak to Zerubbabel son of Shealtiel, governor of Judah, to Joshua son of Jozadak, the high priest, and to the remnant of the people. Ask them, 'Who of you is left who saw this house in its former glory? How does it look to you now? Does it not seem to you like nothing? But now be strong, Zerubbabel,' declares the LORD. 'Be strong, Joshua son of Jozadak, the high priest. Be strong, all you people of the land,' declares the LORD, 'and work. For I am with you,' declares the LORD Almighty. 'This is what I covenanted with you when you came out of Egypt. And my Spirit remains among you. Do not fear'. This is what the LORD Almighty says: 'In a little while I will once more shake the heavens and the earth, the sea and the dry land. I will shake all nations, and what is desired by all nations will come, and I will fill this house with glory,' says the LORD Almighty. 'The silver is mine and the gold is mine,' declares the LORD Almighty. 'The glory of this present house will be greater than the glory of*

*the former house,' says the LORD Almighty. 'And
in this place I will grant peace,' declares the LORD
Almighty".*

I have titled this chapter as "The triple unction". Time
ago, talking to my good friend Manfred Krausse about this subject, he made me note something transcendent that happened in
this occasion. For the first and only time in the history of Israel, a
prophet, a priest and a king worked together for a common project.

The unction of mission

The high priest Joshua, son of Jozadak represents the unction of mission. The most important task a priest had in those
time was to be an intermediary between the people and God, that
is to help the people to live the full life God had prepared for them.

The mission of the whole church is that as individual
Christians to live the plenitude and abundance Christ paid for
each of us, to all become spiritual people, to all reach Christ´s
plenitude and as his children take the good news to those who
still don´t know Jesus. Our mission as a church is to somehow be
intermediaries between men and God, teaching them the way of
finding forgiveness, peace and a full life.

The unction of vision

The unction of vision was an exclusive prophet´s ministry,
in this case Haggai´s. The basic task of a prophet was to bring
people God´s word, indications and strategies to carry out God´s
entrusted work. In this story, God tells Haggai to go with the governor Zerubbabel and the priest Joshua to exhort them about the

reconstruction of the temple.
Chapter 1:12-15 states it like this:

> "*Then Zerubbabel son of Shealtiel, Joshua son of Jozadak, the high priest, and the whole remnant of the people obeyed the voice of the LORD their God and the message of the prophet Haggai, because the LORD their God had sent him. And the people feared the LORD. Then Haggai, the LORD's messenger, gave this message of the LORD to the people: "I am with you," declares the LORD. So the LORD stirred up the spirit of Zerubbabel son of Shealtiel, governor of Judah, and the spirit of Joshua son of Jozadak, the high priest, and the spirit of the whole remnant of the people. They came and began to work on the house of the LORD Almighty, their God, on the twenty-fourth day of the sixth month in the second year of King Darius*".

The exhortation had caused a positive reaction in the governor as well as in the high priest and the remaining people. Obedience brought as a consequence a promise from God saying: "I am with you".

Today, pastors and leaders are the ones who have the prophetic function, that means they create the vision and strategy to carry out the Great Commission. We need to understand that the Great Commission is the same for each church or local congregation, but the vision, the strategy of how to reach that goal may change from congregation to congregation.

We have a very creative God. The easiest thing is to copy

models, see what works in another place and try to adjust it to our local church, but we actually lose the secret of success, which is to find God´s wave in our own context and ride it. No surfer creates his own wave to ride it, what he does is wait by the shore for the perfect wave, ride it and surf. We need to do the same as pastors and leaders, be expectant in prayer, reflection and communion to see which wave God has prepared for our congregation, and ride it. Our job is not to create a wave but to discern what the Father is doing and join Him. We need to understand that we are the Holy Spirit's associates and if we keep a fluent communion, He can reveal us the heart of the Father.

The unction of provision

This unction was reserved for rulers, for those who had power. In this case the governor Zerubbabel gave the orders and put people and resources to gather the necessary materials to carry out the reconstruction of the temple.

If we analyze the word 'provision' we come to realize that it's the result of two combined words: 'Pro' (in favor of) and 'vision'. Therefore, in this context, the governor's job wasn't to question the vision, but to be in favor of it, not only of words, but also with the resources he had at his disposal.

Nowadays, us Christians in general, especially those who have economic, influential resources, gifts, etc. are called or have received the unction of provision. I'm completely convinced that when a church has a clear vision of where it wants to go and how to get there, and it has identified God's wave, then the resources will appear, the provision will come; because God doesn't ask us to do something without the necessary resources.

As Christ's church we are living special times. I would say we are coming back from captivity and there are many things to reconstruct. In the last few years, God has provided to his church of men and women who have a huge responsibility with others to play the roles of prophets and priests, to elaborate God's vision and strategy for the reconstruction of the church, in every sense. We are living in times where God is revealing the original designs of His leaders.

Dear reader, you have been called by God to receive the unction of provision, that is to be one of the agents, governors, Zerubbabels, people through whom the necessary resources for the reconstruction can be provided and I am completely convinced that if you accept this challenge from God, not only will God give you the resources to carry out His will, but will also give you the resources you need.

Which of the three unctions is the most important? All of them; none of them can be carried out independently. As a church we need to take into account these three aspects in the development of our task. The unction of vision, to carry out the unction of mission needs the unction of provision, but the unction of provision without vision or mission simply becomes a church that thinks is alive, but as Jesus says, is dead.

Pray: *"Father, thank you because you gave me gifts, talents, resources, time, etc. I want to be one of the Zerubbabels and governors of these times. I want to give, invest; not only my resources but whatever is in my reach to make a difference in others' lives and your Kingdom. I need YOU for that. I give you all that I am and have for you to use me as you want. In Jesus' name. Amen".*

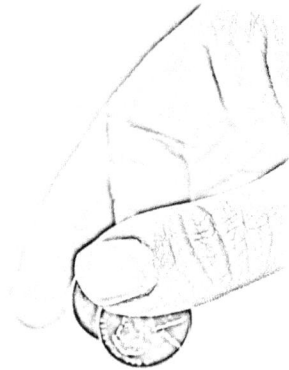

9 – PERSONAL CHALLENGE TO A GENEROUS OFFERING (PCGO)

I understand God establishes through the New Testament that the 100% of what I have and am is His; therefore, I accept HIS challenge of growing in my giving with generosity for HIS cause. I admit that I will never be as generous as God, who gave His son Jesus for my salvation. I propose myself over the year to exceed the scribes and Pharisees' justice, who also gave the 10% of their incomes to God.

Month 1:

With God's grace, I propose myself to joyfully give my offering of the 1% of my incomes, without necessity nor obligation, believing God will surprise me. I take as a challenge the words Jesus declared when he said: *"You have been faithful with a few things; I will put you in charge of many things"*. (Matthew 25:21-23)

Month 2:

With God's grace, I propose myself to joyfully give my o-ffering of the 2% of my incomes, without necessity nor obligation, with the conviction that God deserves the best of me. I take as a challenge the words Jesus declared when he said: *"It will be good for that servant whose master finds him doing so when he returns"*. (Matthew 24:46)

Month 3:

With God's grace, I propose myself to joyfully give my o-ffering of the 3% of my incomes, without necessity nor obligation, with the certainty that I'm sowing in good soil. I take as a cha-llenge the words Jesus declared when he said: *"Still other seed fell on good soil, where it produced a crop—a hundred, sixty or thirty times what was sown"*. (Matthew 13:8)

Month 4:

With God's grace, I propose myself to joyfully give my o-ffering of the 4% of my incomes, without necessity nor obligation, with faith in that God's promises are true. I take as a challenge the words Jesus declared when he said: *"Give, and it will be given to you. A good measure, pressed down, shaken together and running over, will be poured into your lap. For with the measure you use, it will be measured to you"*. (Luke 6:38)

Month 5:

With God's grace, I propose myself to joyfully give my o-ffering of the 5% of my incomes, without necessity nor obligation, understanding that as I pay other expenses, there's a part that belongs to God. I take as a challenge the words Jesus declared when he said: *"So give back to Caesar what is Caesar's, and to God what is God's"*. (Matthew 22:21)

Month 6:

With God's grace, I propose myself to joyfully give my offering of the 6% of my incomes, without necessity nor obligation, agreeing that God doesn't appreciate my leftovers, but my hands' effort. I take as a challenge the words Jesus declared when he said: "Just as he was speaking, Judas, one of the Twelve, appeared. With him was a crowd armed with swords and clubs, sent from the chief priests, the teachers of the law, and the elders. Now the betrayer had arranged a signal with them: *"The one I kiss is the man; arrest him and lead him away under guard"*. (Mark 14:43-44)

Month 7:

With God's grace, I propose myself to joyfully give my offering of the 7% of my incomes, without necessity nor obligation, believing that my giving should be proportional to how I have prospered. I take as a challenge for my life the practice of the three principles established by God through the Apostle Paul, who said: *"On the FIRST DAY of the week let each one of you LAY something ASIDE, storing up as he may PROSPER, that there be no collections when I come"*. (1 Corinthians 16:2)

Month 8:

With God's grace, I propose myself to joyfully give my offering of the 8% of my incomes, without necessity nor obligation, accepting God's challenge to complete in my life His work of grace to transform me in a generous being. I take as a challenge the words God said through the Apostle Paul, who declared: *"For you know the grace of our Lord Jesus Christ, that though he was rich, yet for your sake he became poor, so that you through his poverty might become rich".* (2 Corinthians 8:9)

Month 9:

With God's grace, I propose myself to joyfully give my offering of the 9% of my incomes, without necessity nor obligation, experimenting in my own life that the word God declared is true. I take as a challenge and motto for my life what God declares through the Apostle Paul: *"Each of you should give what you have decided in your heart to give, not reluctantly or under compulsion, for God loves a cheerful giver".* (2 Corinthians 9:7)

Month 10:

With God's grace, I propose myself to joyfully give my offering of the 10% of my incomes, without necessity nor obligation, accepting the pact God makes with His people and believing with faith that what He says is true. I humbly take a challenge what God declares through the prophet Malachi, when he says: *"Bring the whole tithe into the storehouse, that there may be food in my house. Test me in this," says the LORD Almighty, "and see if I will not throw open the floodgates of heaven and pour out so much blessing that there will not be room enough to store it".* (Malachi 3:10)

Month 11:

With God's grace, I propose myself to joyfully give my offering of the 11% of my incomes, without necessity nor obligation, believing God is my Father and that He supplies my needs. I take as a challenge, and with faith, Jesus' words, who declares saying: *"Look at the birds of the air; they do not sow or reap or store away in barns, and yet your heavenly Father feeds them. Are you not much more valuable than they? But seek first his kingdom and his righteousness, and all these things will be given to you as well".* (Matthew 6:26, 33)

Month 12:

With God's grace, I propose myself to joyfully give my offering of the 12% of my incomes, without necessity nor obligation, agreeing with God in the universal principle of sow and harvest. I take as a challenge the words God says through the Apostle Paul, who declares: *"So I thought it necessary to urge the brothers to visit you in advance and finish the arrangements for the generous gift you had promised. Then it will be ready as a generous gift, not as one grudgingly given".* (2 Corinthians 9:5)

From now on, the grace and joy the Holy Spirit gives me, I propose myself to keep growing in my giving with generosity, understanding that what God declares is true, when he says through the Apostle Paul: *"Now he who supplies seed to the sower and bread for food will also supply and increase your store of seed and will enlarge the harvest of your righteousness".* (2 Corinthians 9:10) I admit that the seed I have to sow is actually not mine, but that the Father gives me it to allow me to keep sowing.

Complete name:..

Place:.. Date: ....

CONCLUSION
A CALL TO GENEROSITY

One day a person from a church, at the end of the service, came up to the pastor and said: "Pastor, you do nothing but ask for money; you ask it for Sunday school, for the missions, the sound system, you ask for so many things; it always seems like the church is in need". The pastor, somewhat saddened, answered: "You know brother, I had a son whom I loved very much. I was always spending money for his cause, in food, clothes, shoes, books, courses and much more. But one day he had an illness and passed away. Since then he hasn't cost me anything". The he added: "Brother, each need a church has is a sign of growth. When a church is no longer spending money is because it's dead, do you understand?" The man, a bit ashamed, shook hands with the pastor and apologized.

Concluding, I would like us to meditate a little about a call to generosity God makes us, through the Apostle Paul, so that we can understand that the key to giving is mainly in giving ourselves to the Lord. 2 Corinthians 8:1-15 says:

> *"And now, brothers and sisters, we want you to know about the grace that God has given the Macedonian churches. In the midst of a very severe trial, their overflowing joy and their extreme poverty welled up in rich generosity. For I testify that they gave as much as they were able, and even beyond their ability. Entirely on their own, they urgently pleaded with us for the privilege of sharing in this service to the Lord's people. And they exceeded our expectations: They gave themselves first of all to the Lord, and then by the will of God also to us. So we urged Titus, just as he had earlier made a beginning, to bring also to completion this act of grace on your part. But since you excel in everything—in faith, in speech, in knowledge, in complete earnestness and in the love we have kindled in you—see that you also excel in this grace of giving. I am not commanding you, but I want to test the sincerity of your love by comparing it with the earnestness of others. For you know the grace of our Lord Jesus Christ, that though he was rich, yet for your sake he became poor, so that you through his poverty might become rich. And here is my judgment about what is best for you in this matter. Last year you were the first not only to give but also to have the desire to do so. Now finish the work, so that your eager willingness to do it may be matched by your completion of it, according to your means. For if the willingness is there, the gift is acceptable according to what one has, not according to what one does not have. Our*

desire is not that others might be relieved while you are hard pressed, but that there might be equality. At the present time your plenty will supply what they need, so that in turn their plenty will supply what you need. The goal is equality, as it is written: "THE ONE who gathered MUCH, DID NOT HAVE MUCH and THE ONE who gathered LITTLE, DID NOT HAVE LITTLE".

One of the projects closest to Paul's heart, was the offering he was organizing for the church of Jerusalem. Jerusalem was the mother of all churches, but was going through a time of need because of the drought, and Paul's desire was for gentile churches to remember and help their mother in faith. So in these verses Paul reminds the Corinthians their duty and urges them to be generous. To do so, he uses five resources or arguments to encourage them to give with dignity. These are:

The example of others

Paul shared with them how generous the brothers of the Macedonian churches had been. He tells them they were poor and had problems but that they had given everything they had and much more than what anyone would have expected.

In the Jewish party of purification, there was a rule that said that, as poor a person was, this one should look for someone poorer than themselves, and offer them help. Not always the richest are the most generous. Most times those who have less to give are those who are more willing to do so. There are times that the following quote is very true: "It's the poor who helps the poor", since he knows poverty.

There's a story told about a blind girl in China, who one day brought the pastor 30 shillings for the missionary work. So the pastor said: "You can't give so much". So she answered: "It's true that I'm blind, but I can give these 30 shillings better than anyone else". "How's that?" the pastor asked. She said: "I'm a basket maker and I can work both day and night, and I'm sure that all my other colleagues have spent more than 30 shillings last winter on electricity to work, while I have saved. Therefore, I beg you to take this money for God's work". The second argument Paul used was:

Jesus' example

For Paul, Jesus' sacrifice didn't start at the cross, it didn't even start the day of his Birth in Bethlehem. The sacrifice actually started when he left aside his Glory and accepted to come to Earth and then do everything he did. God's Challenge for your life and mine is the following: "With that tremendous and moving example of generosity in front of us, how can we stay behind? If Jesus gave so much, how can we give less?"

His own past

They had been first in everything, how could they stay behind in this? What a difference there would be if we always lived according to our highest aspirations in the best possible way! We could have as a personal motto never to fall below what we consider the best of us.

Pure feelings put in action

Paul underlines the need to put in action pure feelings.

The Corinthians had been the first to feel the call to that plan. But a feeling that stays feeling, the existing compassion in the heart as it is, an excellent wish that never becomes a beautiful reality, are no more than frustrations. The tragedy of life very often isn't not having good drives, but that many times we leave them as it is and don't make them into actions. We should not only have pure feelings to give, but we should also put in action those noble feelings.

The principle of sow and harvest

Paul reminds them that life has an odd way of equating things. In life we often find that we are measured in the same way we measure others. Life has a way of paying abundance with abundance and the spirit that skimps its equal. The quote in verse 15: *"THE ONE who gathered MUCH, DID NOT HAVE MUCH and THE ONE who gathered LITTLE, DID NOT HAVE LITTLE"* is extracted from Exodus 16:18 where the author states: *"And when they measured it by the omer, the one who gathered much did not have too much, and the one who gathered little did not have too little. Everyone had gathered just as much as they needed".* This text describes the time when Israel was in the desert and gathered the manna every day to eat. No matter if they gathered much or little, it was always enough.

These are the five arguments Paul used to interest us and encourage us to give with generosity. But, besides this, Paul adds something nice about the Macedonians. He points out that they first gave themselves and so they did. In 2 Corinthians 5:8 Paul writes: *"We are confident, I say, and would prefer to be away from the body and at home with the Lord".*

Here we find the secret key of giving generously. That is to give ourselves to the Lord like as a living sacrifice and pleasing to God. Two of them stood out from the rest. There was Aristarchus of Thessalonica, who was with Paul in his last trip to Rome, who during Paul's imprisonment was with him until the end. And there was also Epaphroditus, who, being Paul imprisoned, visited him in jail taking him a generous offering from the church of Philippiand while being there became seriously ill.

No offering can be true unless the giver gives a little of himself with it. That's the reason why the personal offering is always higher and Jesus is the supreme example of this kind of gift. A dead church doesn't need donations, but an alive church that wants to grow and expand, needs the generosity of its people.

Many times we may think "I earn very little to be able to give, those who earn more are better able to give". But it doesn't have to be like that. There's a story told about an old lady who lived in a shack. She had always been a fanatic religious, but since she had had an encounter with Jesus, and had known Him as her personal Lord and Savior, she was happy because she could understand the Gospel on her own.

One day she came to her pastor and told him: "Pastor, the Bible teaches us to give generously, tell me how to do so". The pastor, knowing about her poverty said: "You need more money to buy your medicines, to feed, dress, and take care of yourself. I think God would excuse you". "No", answered the woman. "I want to comply with every spiritual law in its whole. I have to wash clothes to earn money for me, but I have a chicken with eight little chicks. If I gave one of them to the Lord, would that be a generous offering?" The pastor told her it would. Time later, the lady said that the chick she had given to God lamed more eggs than the rest.

She had dedicated God the best, and gave Him the first results. Not surprisingly one of her grandsons, who she maintained in poverty, has now a good job and is an active and generous person in God's work. God blessed abundantly that old lady.

We could be going through difficult times in terms of economy, but I don't think we are at the same level of the churches in Macedone. May God let us give ourselves to Him first and then everything else, and that when someone writes our story or the story of the church where we congregated, they say what Paul said about the Macedonian churches, when he wrote the following: "And now, brothers and sisters, we want you to know about the grace that God has given the Macedonian churches. In the midst of a very severe trial, their overflowing joy and their extreme poverty welled up in rich generosity. For I testify that they gave as much as they were able, and even beyond their ability. Entirely on their own, they urgently pleaded with us for the privilege of sharing in this service to the Lord's people. And they exceeded our expectations: They gave themselves first of all to the Lord, and then by the will of God also to us".

Pray: *"Dear Father, thanks for helping me understand that everything belongs to you. Thanks for this progressive revelation that has reached me. Thank you because I understand that there's no limit for you in terms of what I can give. Make me a generous person, as an answer to your great generosity in sending Jesus, your only Son, to die for me. In Jesus' name. Amen".*